OIL IN THE SOIL

OIL IN THE SOIL

The Politics of Paying to Preserve the Amazon

Pamela L. Martin

ROWMAN & LITTLEFIELD PUBLISHERS, INC.

Lanham • Boulder • New York • Toronto • Plymouth, UK

Published by Rowman & Littlefield Publishers, Inc.
A wholly owned subsidary of The Rowman & Littlefield Publishing Group, Inc.
4501 Forbes Boulevard, Suite 200, Lanham, Maryland 20706
http://www.rowmanlittlefield.com

Estover Road, Plymouth PL6 7PY, United Kingdom

British Library Cataloguing in Publication Information Available

Library of Congress Cataloging-in-Publication Data

Martin, Pamela, 1971–
  Oil in the soil : the politics of paying to preserve the Amazon / Pamela L. Martin.
    p. cm.
  Includes bibliographical references and index.
  ISBN 978-1-4422-1128-5 (cloth : alk. paper) — ISBN 978-1-4422-1130-8 (electronic)
  1. Environmental policy—Ecuador—Parque Nacional Yasuni. 2. Environmental protection—Ecuador—Parque Nacional Yasuni. 3. Environmental degradation—Ecuador—Parque Nacional Yasuni. 4. Petroleum industry and trade—Environmental aspects—Ecuador—Parque Nacional Yasuni. 5. Parque Nacional Yasuni (Ecuador)—Environmental conditions. I. Title.
  TD171.5.E2M376 2011
  333.78'309866416—dc22

                                                                2011010688

∞™ The paper used in this publication meets the minimum requirements of American National Standard for Information Sciences—Permanence of Paper for Printed Library Materials, ANSI/NISO Z39.48-1992.

Printed in the United States of America

To Bill, Gabriella, and William
with much love and admiration

Contents

Acknowledgments

THIS STUDY HAS BEEN a personal journey shared with many family and friends since the inception of my research in 2006, and in many ways reflects years of study of and travel to Ecuador as well. The Yasuní-ITT Initiative and its actors are a constant inspiration to me and a symbol of the changing global politics of our time. While global climate change talks, such as those in Cancun in December 2010, labor slowly with few pathbreaking results, the Yasuní-ITT Initiative stands out as a harbinger for change—one that is not waiting until the world decides to agree on real solutions for the urgent problems that impact our very way of life on this planet. The study of this initiative is also a testament to the authority and power vested in individuals in the global system. Given the pioneering nature of this proposal to leave oil underground in a pristine plot of the Amazon, precedent and other case studies are lacking. This manuscript is an attempt to analyze the challenges of such work and document the processes for replication by other policy makers seeking to enact innovative programs in the hopes of reversing the devastating impacts of climate change.

Earlier versions of sections of this book are published with *Global Environmental Politics*, entitled "Global Governance from the Amazon: Leaving Oil Underground in Yasuní National Park, Ecuador," and an *International Development Policy* contribution entitled "Pay to Preserve: The Global Politics of Ecuador's Yasuní-ITT Proposal." Many of the revisions and much of the continued analysis that are found within this book are owed to exchanges with María Laura Patiño, Grace Jaramillo, and William DeMars at the International Studies Association conference in 2009, as well as a May 2010 panel at the conference on International Economic Rights at La Universidad Andina Simón Bolívar, organized by María Laura Patiño with panelists Juan Fernando Terán and Byron Real, and discussant Martha Roldós. I thank the members of the Analytica Securities meetings on Fridays, in particular Ramiro Crespo, Margarita Andrade, and Rene Ortiz. Close readers of my previous works and this book will note the continued evolution of my ideas and the initiative.

My work on this initiative would never have taken off had it not been for a conversation with Dr. Miranda Schreurs at the American Political Science Association conference in 2005. As I bemoaned the state of the Amazon and its future and my inability to change it, she encouraged me to continue my studies in just such an important area. She was right. I am also deeply grateful to Esperanza Martinez, Acción Ecológica, and Oilwatch International for inviting me to join the toxi-tour of the northern Ecuadorian Amazon in October 2006. While I had been to this area many times before, I had not had such personal contact with its peoples and places. The faces of the children of Shushufindi and the stories of their mothers will forever be engrained in my soul. Many thanks to them for sharing their stories and their struggles.

None of the research for this book would have been possible without the support of the Fulbright Commission and its Fulbright Scholar Award in the spring of 2009. The Ecuadorian Fulbright Commission office welcomed me to the country and made my family at home. My sponsoring institution, La Universidad San Francisco de Quito, and Dr. Carlos Espinoza of the Department of International Relations and his family provided not only academic support, but friendship and collegiality that I will always value. Coastal Carolina University also contributed greatly to my ability to research and write, and it continues to support my scholarship in this area. When I received the Fulbright grant and a coordinating sabbatical to write up my research in the spring of 2008, the full extent of the economic crisis had not yet hit. Yet, even during difficult economic times for our university, Coastal supported my research and writing, and for this I am so grateful. I also owe a debt of gratitude to the Department of Politics and my colleagues, who covered course loads and advising for me while I was away.

Those who contributed to my thoughts are so numerous that I cannot list all of their names. The interviewees listed in this book and those who wished to remain anonymous were invaluable sources of information and constant reminders of the generosity that still exists among people. In all interviews, individuals opened their doors and, in many cases, spent hours talking to me about the environment, energy, politics, and the oil industry in Ecuador and globally. While this book is clearly a study of an initiative that seeks to leave oil underground, it is in no way an indictment against the oil industry and its leaders and workers. Energy is not an easy issue, particularly when its demand is so great and Ecuador's economy depends on it so significantly. While most thought that members of the oil industry would never talk to me, or at least not openly, they were quite wrong. I appreciate the frankness and openness of industry leaders about this initiative and the challenges of the oil industry going forward.

There are some to whom I owe a deep gratitude for sharing their works and ideas with me, and for encouraging me to press on with this project. Alberto Acosta not only provided data in an interview, but he has generously shared his writings, PowerPoint presentations, and e-mail messages that are too numerous to count. His tireless efforts and detailed analyses are nothing short of extraordinary. Esperanza Martínez has over the years opened her office door and shared her thoughts freely with me. Such passion and hard work is a constant source of motivation for me. I thank Federico Starnfeld, who has read (various times) portions of my book and made copious comments on it. Joseph Henry Vogel's work on *The Economics of the Yasuní Initiative* greatly helped frame alternative ideas in my own analysis. I also thank Dr. Vogel for his title suggestion for this book. Matt Finer and Carl Ross of Save America's Forests have provided both invaluable insights from the NGO world and some of the photos in this book. Dr. Finer and his colleagues' studies of this region are the definitive sources of biodiversity data, and they have greatly assisted my understanding of the ecological impacts and importance of Yasuní. These are just a few names, though, of the many who shared interviews and informal conversations with me, to whom I am so grateful.

No manuscript is ever ready after its first draft. For his encouragement, insights, analysis, and copyediting, I owe many hours and much appreciation to Dr. Richard Oliver Collin. I am sure that this book would not have been published without his guidance and optimism. Thank you, Richard, for your mentoring and, above all, your friendship. My dear friend Valentina Padula-Castleberg also read a later version of this book and made valuable comments on it. Thomas Princen encouraged me to continue writing on this subject when I had my doubts. I also owe a debt of gratitude to Andrea Lizarzaburu and Shane Watson, both excellent graduate assistants, who spent hours reviewing my text, transcribing interviews, and formatting this manuscript. Carrie Broadwell-Tkach of Rowman and Littlefield has endured endless e-mail questions and phone calls from me, and has been a source of positive feedback for this book.

While this book and its research has most definitely been a process that has involved numerous individuals, it is my family that has taken on the brunt of the work. I've often said that this book is a "family project." My daughter, Gabriella, attended preschool in Ecuador while I was conducting interviews. My son, William, spent most of his time on my back at seven months old in the beginning of our Fulbright stay in Ecuador as we tracked through some of its most biodiverse places, and even napped while I conducted some interviews. To Gabriella and William, I cannot thank you enough for sharing my passions and the joys of Ecuador and its peoples. Above all, my husband Bill, who has a deep connection to nature and the outdoors, has been a constant source of inspiration and my best sounding board. Bill's photos are throughout this book as well. His passion for the Amazon is demonstrated by the week-long trip he took to Yasuní National Park at the Tiputini Biosphere Reserve of La Universidad San Francisco de Quito to take photos and connect with the place our family has come to know and love. Thanks to Bill too for never complaining when I shut my office door to work and for telling me it's time to take a break. This book is written for Bill, Gabriella, and William in the hopes that it contributes to our understanding of how to create innovative plans to save this wondrous planet.

Pamela L. Martin
Pawleys Island, SC
20 December 2010

Acronyms

CAD	Administrative and Leadership Council
CDM	Clean Development Mechanism
CEPE	Ecuadorian State Petroleum Corporation (Corporación Estatal Petrolera Ecuatoriana)
CERs	Certified Emissions Reductions
CGYs	Yasuní Certificate Guarantees
CI	Conservation International
CNF	National Finance Corporation
DINAPA	The Ministry of the Environment and the National Direction of Environmental Protection (the environmental enforcement institution of the Ministry of Energy and Mines)
EIA	Environmental Impact Assessment
EU ETS	European Union Emissions Trading Scheme
FLACSO	Latin American Faculty of Social Sciences (La Facultad Latinoamericana de Ciencias Sociales)
FMTE	The Fund for Energy Transition Yasuní-ITT
GIZ	German International Cooperation Enterprise
IACHR	Inter-American Commission on Human Rights
IADB	Inter-American Development Bank
ILO	International Labor Organization
ITT	Ishpingo-Tambococha-Tiputini
IUCN	International Union for Conservation of Nature
JI	Joint Initiative
NASA	National Aeronautics and Space Administration
POS	Political Opportunity Structure

REDD	Reducing Emissions from Deforestation and Forest Degradation
SAF	Save America's Forests
SENPLADES	The National Secretariat of Planning and Development (Secretaría Nacional de Planificación y Desarrollo)
UNDP	United Nations Development Programme
UNFCCC	United Nations Framework Convention on Climate Change
USAID	United States Aid for International Development
WRI	World Resources Institute
ZI	*zona intangible*

1

Saving Yasuní and the Planet

Toward a Global Politics of the Good Life

M ANY PEOPLE DREAM of a trip to the exotic Amazon Basin, imagining lush greenery and canopy overhead, the sounds of brightly colored macaws at dusk, and monkeys jumping from tree to tree as they traverse the winding waterways while pink freshwater dolphins jump next to the dugout canoe. While in the Western Amazon—one of the most biodiverse areas of our planet—this is still the reality, it may not be for much longer. The states that comprise this area, in particular Colombia, Ecuador, and Peru, have embarked upon new concessions to drill for oil in these pristine areas of our planet. Embroiled in this scenario are indigenous peoples who live within and from the natural world and do not wish to be contacted. Although the world watched the 2010 BP oil spill in the United States' Gulf of Mexico that spilled about 200 million barrels of oil into rich and sensitive marine areas, little is known about the destruction of what some scientists are claiming to be a bank of humanity and nature, the Western Amazonian region.

This book takes a closer look at the case to save one area of the Amazon, the Ishpingo-Tambococha-Tiputini (ITT) block of Yasuní National Park in Ecuador's Western Amazon. The chapters that follow describe the historical relationship between oil, people, and politics in this country and how years of mobilization through global networks have resulted in unique and innovative plans to save the Amazon and other extremely biodiverse places on our planet that face constant pressures to extract their natural resources to battle poverty and interact in a global economy that functions on the basis of fossil fuels. The Yasuní-ITT Initiative calls upon the world to contribute one half of the estimated $700 million of heavy crude oil revenue from extraction to keep one of its largest oil reserves in the ITT block underground and effectively avoid over 400 million metric tons of carbon emissions. The $350 million of contributions annually for ten years is to be placed in a United Nations Development Programme (UNDP) Trust Fund, called the Ecuador Yasuní-ITT Trust Fund (Yasuní Fund hereafter). Ecuador's left-leaning president, Rafael Correa, is spearheading this audacious international campaign to persuade the developed world to share the environmental responsibility for keeping that oil underground, as Ecuador claims it is the largest contributor to the plan. In an effort to refocus the global climate change debate away from carbon mitigation and absorption and toward conservation and carbon emissions avoidance, Ecuador is proposing to lead fossil fuel–dependent, megadiverse countries out of their resource curse.

Yasuní and the Good Life

The goal of *buen vivir* (the good life) is a concept that appears in the Ecuadorian Constitution of 2008, which provides rights to nature with the goal of achieving harmonious balance between nature and humankind. The Yasuní-ITT Initiative is consistent with such philosophy. It aims to shift the focus of the post-2012 Kyoto Protocol talks away from the developed, industrialized nations and toward the developing ones most affected by climate fluctuations. This study analyzes the complex transnational politics and global governance mechanisms employed to support such normative change. In the global arena, the initiative opens new avenues for support and normative change while constraining state and non-state Ecuadorian actors in established global institutions and mechanisms that support innovative proposals.

The good life is not a utopian dream. The concept has deep and ancient roots in the *cosmovisión* of indigenous peoples, where nature and man coexist in harmony. From this indigenous perspective, equitable and sustainable living has priority over development driven by the neoliberal ideology of markets. Ninety-eight percent of Ecuadorians voted in favor of the constitution passed in Montecristi in 2008. The term in Quichua for the good life is *sumak kawsay* and it has become the backbone of the policies for the constitution. The politics of the good life, which include rights granted to nature, are the driving elements in keeping oil underground and pursuing alternative energy policies in this resource-rich developing country.

The initiative has been called "the crown jewel" of post-Kyoto plans and has been supported by international non-governmental organizations (INGOs), international organizations (IGOs), scientific communities, and celebrities worldwide. Called the Yasuní Man and the Biosphere Reserve under the UNESCO Man and the Biosphere program, this pristine area is one of the hottest of the Earth's biodiverse "hot spots," and it includes two communities who live in voluntary isolation, the Tagaeri and Taromenane. The politics and networks result in complexities for global governance and an uneven pace in new climate change agreements.

As the world ponders its common threat from global climate change, Ecuador is taking action. In June 2007, Ecuadorian president Rafael Correa announced that he would forgo oil profits for one of the country's largest oil reserves (20 percent of its proven reserves) in the Amazonian Yasuní National Park in exchange for contributions from the international community to pay Ecuadorians to keep oil underground. Since his announcement, the Yasuní-ITT (Ishpingo-Tambococha-Tiputini) Initiative has captured the world's imagination and changed to accommodate our current debates about global warming. In many respects, this proposal represents the struggles of all peoples around the globe who seek better, cleaner environments not just for themselves, but for their grandchildren.

If successful, the Yasuní Fund could become the largest global environmental trust fund of its kind. The funds would be directed to protecting Yasuní National Park, improving the lives of those who live within its boundaries, and to developing alternative energy sources for the country. The ultimate objective is to transition Ecuador from an economy dependent upon fossil fuels for its development to a post-petroleum society that focuses on sustainable development and living in harmony with nature, in other words, the politics of *buen vivir*, the good life.

This book will examine the Yasuní-ITT plan and its global governance mechanisms and challenges as it seeks to unite local, indigenous norms of *sumak kawsay*, or the good life—living in harmony with nature—with global concerns of climate change and post-petroleum energy policies. These "avoided emissions" are distinct from the current standards of the Kyoto Protocol, which first only apply to those who have ratified the treaty, and second, apply to already emitted carbon dioxide. Thus, the proposal calls for the inclusion of new, post-Kyoto standards of non-emitted carbon dioxide, and the inclusion of developing countries in the framework of the new international regulations. The projects the government outlines through its National Development Plan apply to current Clean Development Mechanisms (CDM) within the Kyoto Protocol and to the United Nations' Reducing Emissions from Deforestation and Forest Degradation (REDD) program, or possible post-2012 international climate change agreements.[1]

The proposal to save one of the world's most biodiverse areas contains three objectives: 1) to reduce CO2 emissions, 2) to protect biodiversity—including the rights of uncontacted indigenous peoples, and 3) to reduce poverty in Ecuador.[2] While other Amazonian initiatives in South America, such as Brazil's Amazon Fund, call for protection of their forests, this proposal is unique in its social aspects.[3] It combines the normative underpinnings of a post-petroleum Ecuador with socio-environmentalism and the struggle for equitable living within a sustainable environment. Furthermore, President Correa and his Administrative and Leadership Council (CAD) for the initiative are pressing for new solutions in a post-Kyoto climate agreement that includes plans from the developing world and areas, such as Ecuador, that will be severely impacted by climate change. As President Correa enthusiastically announced in one of his Saturday radio addresses, "The success of this project has historic meaning, not just on the level of our country, but internationally."[4] Clearly, the goals of the plan intertwine global and local objectives and norms.

In lieu of oil extraction in this most biodiverse area of our planet, Ecuador is asking the world to donate to a capital fund, invested in fixed income shares. At the time of this writing, the government has signed a Memorandum of Agreement with the United Nations Development Programme (UNDP) to administer the trust fund with the participation of major contributors and representatives of the Ecuadorian government.[5] The funds would be invested in five specific areas of sustainable development which align with the National Development Plan devised by the government.[6] The five areas include: 1) conservation and prevention of deforestation in forty protected areas, totaling 4.8 million hectares, and administration of 5 million hectares of natural areas that belong to indigenous and Afro-Ecuadorian communities; 2) reforestation, forestation, and natural regeneration of 1 million hectares of forest owned by small landholders that are threatened by soil degradation; 3) increased national energy efficiency and expanded renewable energy generation, such as hydroelectric, geothermal, wind, and solar power; 4) social development in the areas of education, health, and training; and 5) support for research, science, technology, and innovation through programs that enhance bio-knowledge, river basin management, and changes in the country's energy matrix.[7]

The Science That Grounds the Initiative

The need to protect tropical rainforests—a vast carbon pool—is ever greater as scientists predict that climate change will melt the world's glaciers and create dry savannah out of the moist and humid Amazon Basin. The planet has changed so dramatically that Nobel Prize–winning chemists Paul Crutzen and Eugene F. Stoermer have declared that we have entered a new geological epoch, which they call the Anthropocene Era.[8] Yet hope awaits if we consider the thermodynamics of the planet, meaning how energy responds to changes in the planetary system. According to Joseph Henry Vogel, "One of the points in that cluster is the Yasuní-ITT Initiative. Thinking thermodynamically, from the bifurcation point of a novel idea can emerge amplification effects on material and energy flows that will determine whole systems."[9]

On June 23, 1988, James Hansen of the National Aeronautics and Space Administration (NASA) announced that the human-caused greenhouse effect was a reality, yet over twenty years later we lack clear and innovative responses to this global crisis. Since then, carbon dioxide emission from fossil fuels has increased over 37 percent, with China outranking the United States as the world's greatest emitter since 2006. In addition, deforestation has contributed to 6.5 billion more tons of carbon dioxide emissions annually and the loss of 13 million hectares of forest cover per year.[10] The damage to the Amazon is irreversible and has reached record proportions. As of 2009, some 20 percent of the Brazilian Amazonian forest has been destroyed. The estimates for Ecuador are around 30 percent, depending on the study referenced.[11] Ecuador is now in second place behind Paraguay for the most deforestation in South America, not an enviable position.[12] James Hansen inveighs, "This is the last chance."[13]

The science is indeed alarming. W. L. Hare estimates that at 2009 levels of carbon dioxide emissions, the Earth's temperature can be expected to rise 4–6 degrees Celsius (7.2–10.8 degrees Fahrenheit) by the end of this century. Even lowering emissions by 80 percent from our current levels will not completely avert the risks the planet faces.[14] Given such grim statistics, we could also expect a loss of 20–80 percent of the Amazon rainforest.[15] For many who have not seen the changes with their own eyes, it is hard to imagine. But some simple facts make clear the devastation. Thomas Lovejoy, world-renowned biodiversity expert, reminds us that in 2005 Brazil's Amazon experienced a drought—the greatest in recorded history for the region. Some climate models predict that this will continue to occur as temperatures rise and the cycle of rain generation from the Atlantic Ocean to the rainforest diminishes.[16]

Yet natural resource extraction in this fragile environment continues unabated. In fact, it has actually accelerated since the 1970s. Brazil, Colombia, Ecuador, Peru, Venezuela, and Bolivia all have petroleum, natural gas, and mining reserves. Oil, coal, and natural gas account for 86.5 percent of worldwide primary energy sources.[17] While the financial crisis of 2008–2009 seems to have lowered energy needs temporarily, most experts predict that emerging market economies will industrialize with fossil fuel sources for the foreseeable future. Demand will outpace supply with an increase in oil prices and concomitant carbon dioxide.[18] Emissions from the developing world are 55 percent of the worldwide total. The statistic highlights the need to implement renewable sources worldwide. Failure to do so puts at risk places like Yasuní.

Given the rising global demand, countries have increased fossil fuel extraction in the last twenty years. Unfortunately, the countries blessed and cursed by natural resources overwhelmingly rank among the poorest, most corrupt, and least democratic. Of the countries considered in danger of political conflict by the International Crisis Group, 35 percent are oil- and gas-exporting countries.[19] Thomas Friedman and Michael Ross have documented an inverse correlation between the rising price of oil and the level of democratization of a country whose GDP is petroleum-dependent.[20]

Ecuador and the Pipeline

Ecuador is a glaring example of a petro-state. Its oil exports are 35 percent of its $108.2 billion gross domestic product (GDP). It is eleventh on the list of countries that export oil to the United States and it produces approximately 486,000 barrels of oil per day. Its thirty-seven-year run of petroleum extraction has left the country among the poorest in South America, with poverty rates increasing to 45 percent until 2001, and then declining by 20 percent until 2006. However, poverty where oil is abundant—the Amazon—is at extreme levels.

As noted in table 1.1, the Amazon suffers from much higher levels of poverty at 66.8 percent, compared to its neighboring Highland provinces at 43.6 percent and the Coastal provinces at 52.4 percent. Furthermore, cancer rates in oil-producing areas of the Amazon are 31 percent, whereas the national average is 12.3 percent.[21]

Alberto Acosta, the former minister of energy and mines and president of the 2008 Constituent Assembly, argues that the overriding issue facing the Amazon is the violence that has surged since oil development began in the Northern Amazon in 1972. He cites over twelve cases of violent confrontation between local communities and/or indigenous peoples, oil companies, and the military. One conflict in Sarayacu is ongoing and has remained unresolved since 2003. As an economist, Acosta identifies the Ecuadorian Amazon in the taxonomy of Raúl Prebisch, "the periphery of peripheries."[22]

Ecuador is no stranger to oil development. It began its foray into the black gold exploration and extraction off its coast in Santa Elena in 1909 with a contract to an Ecuadorian family under the Concepción Ecuador Oil Company, which was later sold to a British Company, Carlton Granville Dunn. Explora-

TABLE 1.1
Poverty Percentages by City and Region: 1995–2006

	1995	1998	1999	2006
Quito	27.3	19.9	29.1	20.9
Guayaquil	34.6	40.2	47.9	36.0
Coast	51.6	58.4	62.8	52.4
Highland	52.4	53.0	59.3	43.6
Amazon	71.5	63.2	—	66.8
Rural	76.5	77.9	81.6	72.7
Urban	36.3	40.6	47.0	35.6
National Total	52.6	56.3	61.1	49.1

Source: Carlos Larrea, Ana Isabel Larrea, and Ana Lucia Bravo, "Petróleo, sustentabilidad y desarrollo en la Amazonía ecuatoriana: Dilemas para una transición hacia una sociedad post-petrolera," 2008, unpublished manuscript. See also Instituto Nacional de Estadística y Censos (INEC), Encuesta de Condiciones de Vida, 1995, 1998, 1999, 2006 (www.inec.gov.ec).

tion of oil in the Amazon began in 1937 by Royal Dutch Shell under its affiliate Anglo Saxon Petroleum Company Limited, but was soon abandoned. Large-scale exploration and extraction did not begin until 1971 when Texaco Oil Company of the United States entered the Lago Agrio region. In this same year, the first Hydrocarbon Law was passed, creating the legal-institutional structures to support natural resource extraction. By 1974, the Corporación Estatal Petrolera Ecuatoriana (CEPE) was formed and was part of a consortium with Texaco-Gulf.[23]

Currently, 65 percent of Ecuador's Amazon is zoned for oil activities. Since the oil boom of the 1970s, multiple partnerships have formed between the state oil company, now called Petroecuador, and transnational oil companies. The country boasts two oil pipelines that traverse its Amazonian rainforest over the Andes Mountains to the coast. These activities have not gone without conflict, as will be discussed in the following chapters. Most notably, the lasting environmental impact of Texaco (now Chevron-Texaco) in the Northern Amazon is still to be determined by a court of law in Lago Agrio, Ecuador. Suffering from oil spills and seepage into groundwater systems, local and indigenous peoples filed a multibillion-dollar lawsuit against Chevron-Texaco in New York in 1993. The case was moved to Ecuador in 2003 and awaits judgment.

PHOTO 1.1
Oil seepage into the northern Ecuadorian Amazon, near Lago Agrio.

Down River

Disasters from exploration for oil are not confined to the developing world. One thinks of BP and the Gulf of Mexico or Exxon and Valdez, Alaska, for example. Ecuador's Yasuní-ITT Initiative is emblematic of the challenges we all face on the planet. The funding received from the world community would be directed to programs that 1) protect Yasuní National Park; 2) improve the indigenous and non-indigenous communities of the Park; 3) conserve the natural protected areas in the country; 4) create social and economic programs that alleviate poverty in the zones of influence; and 5) fund alternative energy sources, such as hydro, solar, and geothermal alternatives which are all promising in Ecuador. Compared to the other Amazon Fund in Brazil, the Yasuní-ITT Initiative is more holistic—where holism is defined as integrating social and economic development in addition to alternative energy investment, rather than just concentrating on decreasing deforestation, as does the Brazilian Amazon Fund. While the Yasuní-ITT Initiative has the potential to integrate other funding mechanisms to achieve its goals, such as REDD and CDM programs, it emphasizes the global contributions toward holistic sustainable development for the country to move it away from its fossil fuel dependence.[24] Ecuadorian government officials contend that they would like to lead the world toward another model of sustainable development, eventually making their country a "green pioneer."

The Yasuní-ITT global campaign has not been without its ebbs and flows of controversy. Chapter 2 will examine the nexus of local, national, and global advocacy networks that have formed and how we can view them in a new lens that fits what we are observing in advocacy networks from the South. While the 1990s brought a plethora of data and evidence that suggested northern NGOs were connecting and collaborating with southern NGOs to form a "boomerang effect" and change violating states' policies, this case demonstrates a change.[25] The actors in this case are primarily southern-based NGOs who have worked since the 1990s to develop alternative norms about natural resource extraction and sustainable development. It is their advocacy, mobilization, and struggle that has inspired and motivated the Yasuní-ITT Initiative. Northern NGOs, while significant in the mobilization, respond to the southern claims rather than try to form their own. Thus, any depiction of an evil and rapacious state would not fit. In Ecuador, the state is working with NGOs on the proposal at local, national, and international levels. The emphasis on the advocacy of actors contributes to our understanding of who is truly governing in the complex and varied processes of global governance.

Chapter 3 examines the interconnected histories of oil, environmental rights, and indigenous rights in the Amazon, most particularly in Yasuní

National Park. The issues go beyond the ITT block to global arenas, from transnational oil company struggles to a vibrant international and national environmental NGO advocacy movement, and include local and global struggles to protect some of our planet's most vulnerable communities—the Taromenane and Tagaeri indigenous peoples who remain uncontacted in isolation within the park. The Yasuní-ITT proposal is based on these intricately woven histories and on learning from previous Amazonian experiences of destruction and degradation to the north of this block. Finally, the chapter analyzes the foundations of the proposal through the words of the actors themselves. It illustrates the process of creating alternative norms for a post-petroleum Ecuador and follows the institutional development of such norms through the formulation of the proposal in the context of governmental and non-governmental structures. While some scholars have analyzed various aspects of the proposal from their discipline, no scholarship to date examines why and how the Yasuní-ITT proposal came to life and became official Ecuadorian foreign policy, as well as a subject on the global agendas of NGOs, the European Union, and the United Nations.

Following the launch of the proposal, chapter 4 analyzes the current call to the world through a review of governmental decrees about Yasuní-ITT, the Yasuní-ITT Trust Fund, and in-depth interviews with the actors involved. The initiative reflects the philosophy of the Ecuadorian actors who created it as well as collaborating states. The multiple governmental mechanisms formed to collect contributions and sell avoided emission certificates, called Yasuní Guarantee Certificates (CGYs for their Spanish version), illustrate how actors exert authority to influence policy outcomes. Yasuní-ITT is unique and pathbreaking for global governance institutions, which may set a precedent for other fossil fuel–dependent, megadiverse, and carbon-rich but economically poor countries.[26] While natural scientists have praised the proposal as an innovative solution to global climate change, students of global politics and international relations have much to learn from its iterations and final version. For example, it is significant to note that Ecuador has chosen to route the initiative through the United Nations Framework Convention on Climate Change (UNFCCC), which aligns with the initiative's emphasis on avoided carbon emissions. Indeed, this route is more profitable, particularly given the potential $100 billion Climate Change Fund agreed upon in Cancun in 2010. However, the protection of Yasuní's biodiversity would seem to also make the initiative applicable to the Convention on Biological Diversity (CBD).[27] The actors involved in this process shopped the international environmental forums, which highlights the importance of framing the issue correctly at the international level. Given the complexity of the processes and forums, the Yasuní-ITT Initiative illustrates the significance of actors in the global governance process and the need for scholars of international relations to create more dynamic models to better understand the intricacies of policy formation at multiple levels.

In order to better understand the norms that underpin the proposal and the struggles of actors, chapter 5 examines the proposal through the words of the actors themselves. While such discourse is present throughout this book, only here are motivations and social networks expressed in the words of the actors. Many have assumed that oil company executives were watering at the mouth to gain access to the ITT block and so some may be most surprised to hear the words of oil company representatives. Their opinions differ and their governmental networks differ, yet their discourse underscores the importance of not using a broad brush to paint the motives of the oil companies. In fact, the actors from oil, like those from NGOs and government, view the Yasuní-ITT issue distinctly and some have even created alternative proposals. The significant finding of this chapter is that social learning and networks are catalysts for action. Institutionalization of norms is a varied and messy process with bargaining and debate even among allied network members.

The final analysis in chapter 6 of this book links the original arguments about normative processes and global governance with actors at the forefront of the Yasuní-ITT proposal. I analyze the contributions of the proposal to visions of a post-Kyoto climate change agreement and the challenges that lie ahead for the leaders who are seeking support for it. The ITT block is still not safe from oil extraction as the Ecuadorian government has made it clear that drilling in the block might be necessary if funding to keep oil underground is not found. One might question Ecuador's motives and wonder whether it ultimately plans to drill for oil anyway. However, after many formal and informal interviews through on-ground and virtual (Skype) conferences, the commitment of the leaders of the presidential Administrative and Leadership Council (CAD) who represent the proposal is unwavering and passionate. While not easily quantifiable, the dedication of those involved in this proposal is inspiring. Even those who expressed doubts hope for its success for the sake of the pristine park in which the ITT block lies and communities which have lived there for centuries or millennia.

As a student of global politics, I have studied and visited Ecuador over the span of fourteen years. The country has undergone immense governmental turmoil until the recent election in 2006 of Rafael Correa. The Yasuní-ITT Initiative may be a turn toward a sustainable future for upcoming generations of Ecuadorians and serve as a pilot project for others in the developing world. Regardless of the outcome, the initiative provides scholars and policy makers with answers about how to frame local and global policy issues and move them through the international system. The story and its processes are a testament to the abilities of unknown actors from a small, impoverished country and their search to create the good life for future generations on our planet.

Notes

1. UN-REDD Programme Fund, "Secretary-General and Prime Minister of Norway Launch UN-REDD Programme," http://www.undp.org/mdtf/un-redd/overview.shtml.

2. Carlos Larrea et al., "Yasuní- ITT Initiative a Big Idea from a Small Country," October 2009, http://www.yasuni-itt.gov.ec/download/Yasuni_ITT_Initiative1009.pdf, p. 6.

3. Thomson Reuters Foundation, "Norway Pledges $1 Billion to Brazil Amazon Fund," September 16, 2008; Amazon Fund, "The Amazon Is the Lungs of the Planet: As the Amazon Goes, So Goes the Planet," http://www.amazonfund.org/index.php (accessed October 25, 2009).

4. "Proyecto ITT Avanza Maravilloso, dice Correa," Diario Hoy, May 30, 2009, http://www.hoy.com.ec/noticias-ecuador/proyecto-itt-avanza-maravilloso-dice-correa-351083.html (translation by author).

5. Carlos Larrea, "Resumen expo COICA," August 20, 2009, http://www.youtube.com/watch?v=tqRCOiZTfNo.

6. In 2004, president Rafael Correa instituted the "Secretaría Nacional de Planificación y Desarrollo" (SENPLADES) as the technical organization responsible for national social and economic development planning. SENPLADES is based on the "Plan Nacional de Desarrollo." It is the document that identifies the main development problems and the alternatives to address them. Technical groups from different cabinet ministries collaborated in the formulation of the plan, which was, ultimately, revised by civil consultation.

7. Larrea et al., "Yasuní-ITT Initiative a Big Idea," p. 7; Ecuador Yasuní ITT Trust Fund: Terms of Reference, July 28, 2010, p. 5.

8. Christopher Flavin and Robert Engelman, "The Perfect Storm," in *2009 State of the World: Into a Warming World: A Worldwatch Institute Report on Progress toward a Sustainable Society*, edited by Linda Starke (New York: W. W. Norton, 2009), 5.

9. Joseph Henry Vogel, *The Economics of the Yasuní Initiative: Climate Change as if Thermodynamics Mattered* (London: Anthem Press, 2009), 10.

10. Flavin and Engelman, "Perfect Storm," 6–7.

11. Jefferson Mecham, "Causes and Consequences of Deforestation in Ecuador," Centro de Investigación de los Bosques Tropicales (CIBT), May 2001; Sven Wunder, *The Economics of Deforestation: The Example of Ecuador* (Basingstoke, UK: Macmillan Press, 2000).

12. Wunder, *Economics of Deforestation*.

13. Flavin and Engelman, "Perfect Storm," 7.

14. W. L. Hare, "A Safe Landing for the Climate," in *2009 State of the World: Into a Warming World: A Worldwatch Institute Report on Progress toward a Sustainable Society*, edited by Linda Starke (New York: W. W. Norton, 2009), 13.

15. Hare, "Safe Landing," 20.

16. Thomas Lovejoy, "Climate Change's Pressures on Biodiversity," in *2009 State of the World: Into a Warming World: A Worldwatch Institute Report on Progress toward a Sustainable Society* edited by Linda Starke (New York: W. W. Norton, 2009), 67.

17. Al Gore, *Our Choice: A Plan to Solve the Climate Crisis* (Emmaus, PA: Rodale Publishers, 2009), 57.

18. Global Carbon Project, "Carbon Budget and Trends 2007," September 26, 2008, http://www.globalcarbonproject.org.

19. Jill Shankleman, *Oil, Profits, and Peace: Does Business Have a Role in Peacemaking?* (Washington, D.C.: United States Institute of Peace, 2006), 4.

20. Thomas L., Friedman, "The First Law of Petropolitics," *Foreign Policy*, May-June 2006, 29–36; Michael L. Ross, "Does Oil Hinder Democracy?" *World Politics* 53, no. 3 (April 2001): 325–361.

21. Alberto Acosta, *La Maldición de la Abundancia* (Quito, Ecuador: Abya Yala, 2009), 75.

22. Acosta, *La Maldición de la Abundancia*, 82–86.

23. Acosta, *La Maldición de la Abundancia*, 37–40.

24. Ecuador Yasuní ITT Trust Fund: Terms of Reference 2010, 5.

25. Margaret E. Keck and Kathryn Sikkink. *Activists beyond Borders: Advocacy Networks in International Politics* (Ithaca, NY: Cornell University Press, 1998).

26. The World Conservation Monitoring Centre of the United Nations Environment Programme (UNEP) has designated seventeen megadiverse countries on the planet. Ecuador is one of them.

27. Joseph Henry Vogel, e-mail message to author, 2010.

2

Global Politics from the Canopy

I N THE HEART OF the Andes Mountains and the Amazon Basin, global governance and international campaigns are alive and well. Natural resource extraction in a country like Ecuador provides a lens through which to view the multi-layered global dynamics of international, national, and local campaigns to prevent oil extraction in Ecuador's Amazonian Yasuní National Park. As elsewhere in the world, the Ecuadorian anti–oil extraction movements are part of the global offensive driven by international environmental NGOs. Yet anti–oil extraction movements in Ecuador also have local roots, actors, and agendas that interact with those of global NGOs. The arenas of global and local contestation in the battle to keep oil underground in the ITT block of Yasuní National Park are varied.

While the Ecuadorian state has embraced local NGOs' environmental agendas, it has also institutionalized the proposal to keep oil underground and become its representative at the global level. Yet the Ecuadorian government has also considered new bids for oil extraction within Yasuní National Park. Thus, the transnational campaign to keep oil underground in Yasuní National Park has become both the victim and the benefactor of global governance mechanisms and institutions. NGOs that support the proposal find themselves in the precarious position of both supporting the proposal and the government that is representing it at the global level, yet also being at odds with a government that has criticized them for being "infantile" and against progress because they have impeded the government's attempts to develop further the extraction of oil and the mining resources in the Amazon. Additionally, this movement infuses norms of environmental rights and the indigenous concept of *sumak kawsay*, or *el buen vivir* (the good life), from Ecuador's new constitution passed in 2008 and, at the global level, aims to transform global environmental governance to one that fosters harmony between man and nature.

Global governance is not only the interaction of state institutions and NGOs, but also the market and its actors, namely multinational corporations. In this case, oil companies are part of the Ecuadorian government's Plan B: to drill for oil in the ITT block if funding to keep it underground is not found. Plan B places those actors in favor of keeping oil underground in competition with oil companies and the governmental institutions that support oil extraction, such as the Ministry of Non-Renewable Resources and the state-run oil company, Petroecuador. Thus, the Yasuní-ITT campaign is illustrative of the complex dance between developing countries' traditional government institutions that seek profit from natural resources and those institutions, such as the Ministry of the Environment and environmental NGOs, that seek new forms of energy and environmental governance.

Whatever the arenas of conflict, the sovereign state continues to play a crucial role in shaping the dynamics and the outcome of natural resource conflicts. The role that the state plays goes beyond preventing or ignoring local demands and forcing local actors to transfer their claims to international arenas. In this analysis, I follow the observations of Matthias Finger and "problematize the role of the state" as an institution (albeit authoritative in natural resource issues) among many in the multiple layers of global governance.[1] Amid the general leftward movement in Latin American politics, the state can become more receptive to campaigns against transnational corporations (TNCs), even an ally. In the Yasuní National Park protection campaign, the state has adopted a cause initiated originally by national NGOs and later joined by global NGO coalitions. However, the state is also playing the role of antagonist by soliciting licenses for oil block concessions within Yasuní National Park and limiting the voices and ideas of the original pioneers of the proposal—the environmental and indigenous rights organizations.

International norms also come into play in these conflicts over natural resource policy. Notions of environmental debt swaps, the carbon trade, social justice, and equality all provide signposts for the international regulation of extractive industries. In the Yasuní case, the Correa government is building on traditional international environmental regimes to present an innovative proposal, based on concepts of social environmental rights. The initiative additionally proposes a change in the origin of such norms from northern, industrialized countries that were responsible for the Kyoto Protocol, to southern, developing countries (in this case Ecuador). This directional switch has inspired norm formation from the perspective of the developing world with an emphasis on avoided emissions and rights to nature over the current northern-developed concepts of emissions absorption, sequestration, and mitigation.

This study looks at the anti–oil extraction movement in Yasuní National Park to gauge the composition of transnational advocacy, how its agendas are defined, the arenas in which claims are presented, and the mechanisms of global governance that are established. It intersects the literatures on 1) globalization, 2) non-state actors and transnational networks, 3) social movements, and 4) global governance in order to develop a model of strategy, mobilization, and policy outcomes that crosses the territorial divides of space and place.

International Relations and Globalization: A View from the Rainforest Canopy

Scholars of international relations have long debated the centrality of the role of the state in world politics. While some within the discipline argue cogently

PHOTO 2.1
A view of the rainforest canopy from Yasuní National Park.

that a strong state will only get stronger within the process of globalization,[2] others believe that the system is moving away from a state-dominated structure to include networks of actors that connect local and global levels.[3] These studies call for an examination of global governance in order to improve our analysis of the dynamics and interactions that simultaneously occur at both macro and micro levels. Hall and Chase-Dunn further call for theories that analyze social change at the global level as theories based on local, national, or international levels fall short of connecting the systemic patterns and processes that change policy and inspire movements.[4]

Viewing international processes from the optic of the rainforest canopy can be a useful tool. As some scholars note, the Amazon is a unique region of the world, not only for its biological diversity and carbon sequestration properties, but also for its amalgamation of global and local political, economic, and social challenges.[5] Living within steps of one another, oil companies and indigenous communities interact, for example, within local and national political structures that concomitantly promote the extraction of hydrocarbons and grant constitutional rights to nature and indigenous peoples. Economist and former minister of energy and mines Alberto Acosta argues that the pressures on the Amazon are global, transnational companies and international financial concerns pressure on the national government to capitalize its natural resources and trade them on the free market.[6] At the same time, the significance of the Amazon to abating and mitigating carbon in a global climate change policy is clear. Thus, Acosta calls for policies of *glocalization* that view the local Amazonian needs in light of global demands and solutions. When asked who is responsible for the Yasuní-ITT campaign and its development, he commented, "It is a wide-ranging collectivity. I would say that you cannot look for owners here, rather many people commented on it, gave suggestions, criticisms, etc. . . . This is not a proposal just for Ecuadorians, but for all people on the planet. I think it is truly revolutionary."[7]

Brazil's Amazonian region also displays the role of transnational social movement actors in bringing local issues to global levels. Ken Conca argues that in the Brazilian Amazon the "state is in retreat" in some cases and that pressures in the Amazon have global and local causes and responses.[8] Traditional territorial divisions among state, local, and international levels do not reflect the dynamic interaction among actors at all levels when referring to global environmental movements and policies in the Amazon. Thus, when searching for solutions to these issues, actors organize at local levels with local concerns, norms, and ideas, yet work in tandem with global partners for goals at both levels. This process is indicative of Rosenau's *fragmegration*[9] due to the transnational capital pressures on these resource-rich areas that create local social conflicts, as noted by Sklair.[10]

However, the transnational networks that I outline demonstrate fluidity among the levels with more pressure from southern NGOs and actors on northern NGOs and actors than we have observed in the past. Previous global social movement studies emphasized networks connecting North and South, but with norms and funds flowing from the North toward the South, even if strong communication between the two was observed.[11] This study sheds light on more recent processes that we attribute to learning[12] and capacity building[13] from the 1990s, plus increased participation of southern activists in global processes (such as the World Social Forum), including conferences, networks, and funding sources (such as recent conversations among leaders and southern NGO activists about a Bank of the South in South America).

The Role of Global Governance

For our purposes then, scholarship on global governance and transnational networks offers a lens through which we can usefully view global Amazonian and resource extraction campaigns. Scholars of global governance[14] argue that the traditional approach to the study of international institutions and change (including regime analysis by Krasner)[15] lacks a profound understanding of the porous nature of borders, particularly in the environmental arena. They call for research that examines both the transnational drivers of these problems and their local dynamics. According to Lipschutz and Tetreault, we should study the agency of social action to understand the global/local implications of change, rather than focus exclusively on the state-based structure of the international system.[16] Given the nature of this campaign and its local and global dynamics and implications, this project seeks to create a dynamic model for analyzing processes that do not necessarily originate at the state level and are influenced by a myriad of actors and norms at all levels.

In their illuminating work on Brazil's environmental politics, Hochstetler and Keck observe that the domestic and international are often "intertwined" and that "a framework focusing on the formation of networks in multi-level governance helps to make sense of the many interactions among levels of governance and kinds of actors."[17] That said, I concur with their observation and that of Sidney Tarrow that domestic factors are significant in the process of global governance.[18] In this case, they not only determine the policy outcomes, but also are responsible for the normative origins of this campaign and its institutional developments. The chaotic and *turbulent* processes that form these campaigns are most certainly on Rosenau's frontiers of the domestic and the global, with each interaction contributing to the strategies of the campaign, the makeup of the actors, and the ultimate policy outcomes and governance structures.[19]

Differentiating government from governance provides the enhanced vision of political and normative processes that influence this initiative and its possible outcomes at various levels in the global system.[20] While government entails a state-based hierarchy of authority, governance encompasses states *and* non-state actors in the public and private realms. In the case of oil extraction, the state intermingles with non-state actors and, at points, allows non-state institutions leadership in the coordination and development of the campaigns. Such interaction within these chaotic processes has formed differing levels of authorities at different points for non-state actors within the campaigns. Where I note the highest level of authority for non-state actors in the process is during times of information sharing and capacity building.[21] During the stage of rule setting, particularly in cases of resource extraction, the state is the ultimate purveyor of law, although it is not free from significant input from non-state public and private actors, as the Yasuní-ITT Initiative will demonstrate.[22]

Particularly in the case of Yasuní, the traditional emphasis on the institutional interactions of global governance lacks depth due to its failure to account for the web of social interactions that created and continue to form the campaigns. As James Rosenau puts it, "People Count!"[23] More importantly, the issues of nature and society are boundless and require a de-territorialization of theories, as Ken Conca contends in his "social theory of institution building."[24] The actors within these campaigns have moved in and out of state government, the private sector, and NGOs. They have known each other for years, networked at conferences globally, and researched and published in these areas. It is their ideas and social relations that often impact the campaigns in varied ways. The network-building skills that they have developed throughout their careers, combined with the technology to instantly chat live, converse live via voice-over-Internet-protocol (VOIP), and videoconference live have enhanced their interactions. In the case of the global South, and Ecuador in particular, the availability of Internet access and cell phones has dramatically increased, which has also provided new platforms of exchange among actors who were previously disconnected, most notably in Amazonia.[25]

Networks and Norms

The agency of the actors in these global governance networks is based on their normative underpinnings and ideas. Contrary to network theories that create unidimensional pictures of the formations of global governance networks, I contend that these interactions are not without conflict and negotiation. Open discussion, criticism, and contested negotiation are standard mechanisms of development of the policies that these networks ultimately produce and campaign on. The Yasuní-ITT Initiative is not neatly aligned with current international regimes and norms on oil extraction regulation, but rather pushes the limits of these structures in order to seek change, such as post-Kyoto standards for climate change governance, rather than international regulation of it. The difficulties of funding the Yasuní-ITT proposal to keep oil underground originate from Ecuador's desire to change the current global climate change mechanisms, such as the World Bank Global Environment Facility (GEF), or funding avoided emissions.

In their study of various global governance networks, Khagram and Ali found that "contested transnational structuration processes now more visibly involved multiple sets of actors attempting to enact novel scripts of norms, principles, rules and decision making procedures that could very well be signaling a longer-term shift away from government-centric interstate regimes."[26] While the Ecuadorian government plays a key role as owner of subsoil rights, changes in the regime toward openness to new social movements, most specifically environmental movements, have created opportunity structures for new ways of looking at economic, political, and social development in the country. Thus, I concur with Okereke that "agency is located in structure, but not determined by it."[27] In fact, one of the slogans of the Ecuadorian government's Administrative and Leadership Council (CAD) on the Yasuní-ITT Campaign is to "think outside the box" to create new options to save Yasuní and devise a post-Kyoto climate change policy; in other words, "from Kyoto to Quito."[28]

The normative underpinnings of campaigns are crucial to the understanding of the policy outcomes and new global governance structures that they propose. For that reason, scholarship on constructivist perspectives of international relations best reveals mechanisms of network formation and change via normative and idea processes.[29] These studies have focused primarily on human rights issues, but the study of energy, natural resource, and conservation issues would shed light on the implications of the constructivist approach in other areas.

Norms and principles in the international system are often studied through the lens of non-state actors, including non-governmental organizations (NGOs). Scholars who study these actors have found power in their ability to leverage international norms and opinions against abusive states to reform policies on local levels.[30] Scholars who criticize these actors often cite their market-based behavior and their dependence on the state to function and operate. Part of the equation of mobilization around the Yasuní-ITT campaign is the role of NGOs and their strategies. However, the norms that motivate their agency are built around Ecuadorian-specific concepts of *sumak kawsay* in Quichua, *buen vivir* in Spanish, or *the good life* in English.

Other normative foundations around these issues are social environmental-
ism, ethical ecology, and already established international norms of protected areas for uncontacted indigenous peoples, as well as the protection of
UNESCO Man and the Biosphere sites.[31] Thus, the ideas and norms driving
this campaign weave indigenous *cosmovisión* (worldview) with global norms
from international institutions.

The Good Life

Ecuador's justification for this campaign is based on its new constitution,
passed in September 2008, which is the first to give rights to nature and begin
to define the concept of "*el buen vivir.*" Former President of the Constituent
Assembly, Alberto Acosta explains that this term derives from indigenous
groups and cannot be defined as a linear concept of development in Western
standards, but rather as "a category that is in permanent construction and
reproduction." He adds,

> In it life itself is at stake. Following this holistic concept, from the diversity of
> elements that condition human actions that bring the Good Life, material goods
> are not the only determining factors. There are other values at play, such as:
> knowledge, social and cultural recognition, ethical and even spiritual codes of
> conduct in relation to society and Nature, human values, a vision of the future,
> among others. The Good Life constitutes a central category in the philosophy of
> life for indigenous societies.[32]

The good life also encompasses norms based on ethical ecology as understood by scholar-activists such as Eduardo Gudynas, who argues that politics,
conceived as the democratic mobilization and decision making of people
around the world, are central to saving our planet. For Gudynas, people
should see themselves as part of nature, rather than dominate it. This aligns
with the indigenous *cosmovisión* of nature in which humans are part of the
cycle of the planet, rather than an anthropocentric view of nature.[33]

Moreover, Gudynas questions the role of the scientific community in creating policies that reflect the good life. He argues that scientific findings have
become the justification for policies that defend the environmental impacts
of mining, for example. Instead, such decisions should reflect society and its
multiple values and cultures.[34] The decisions about sustainable development
(and he argues for a strong policy to protect nature) should be made by a
global citizenry to protect the planet. Interestingly, he places people as central
to the politics of nature, but not to nature itself, as it is a process that has its
own cycles and includes all life forms.

The call for global political action in the name of saving the planet and reducing global climate change has been echoed by ecological economist Herman Daly,[35] Yale professor James Gustave Speth,[36] and author-activists Bill McKibben[37] and Paul Hawken.[38] These works emphasize the role of social movements and global citizens in the global governance of climate change. Where the normative underpinning for anti–oil extraction movements becomes less clear is in the economic realm. Here, scholars differ on the value of nature. In other words, can you put a price on the good life?

While Gudynas and Acosta have both argued that there is no price to be placed on protecting nature,[39] other scholars argue that strict environmental regulation, enforcement, and market-based strategies are the keys to preserving our planet.[40] The debate in the U.S. Congress on cap-and-trade systems and the European Union Emissions Trading Scheme (EU ETS) illustrates the prevalence of this conversation in the North, while the story of Yasuní National Park highlights the urgency of policy solutions and a need for consideration of the norms that ground them in the South. This urgency of ideas from the South is reflected in recent scholarship on "new rights advocacy."[41] New rights advocates not only challenge current global policies, such as development mechanisms or climate change, but also provide alternative ideas and policies. Nelson and Dorsey contend that such alternatives are increasingly taking shape from the South and moving into dialogs in transnational networks and international negotiations.[42]

Yet there is common ground among scholars from the North and the South on issues of the environment and development. Northern researchers such as Thomas Princen, Ken Conca, Michael Maniates, and Tim Jackson concur with Southern researchers like Gudynas and Acosta that today's levels of consumerism in the developed world have created unsustainable impacts on the planet.[43] Princen calls for policies that include "sufficiency," rather than accelerated production and consumption.[44] While "sufficiency" is not the same as "avoided emissions," it is in line with the concept of living within our natural environment, rather than exploiting it. The "logic of sufficiency" also aligns with the Ecuadorian concept of *buen vivir* in its promotion of balance within nature. For Thomas Princen sufficiency is "a sense of enoughness and too muchness."[45] This logic requires an understanding that the world is filled with finite resources. Thus, maximizing utility within a finite planet, the cornerstone of economic and political theories, is illogical. As the authors of the book *El Ecuador Post Petrolero* conclude, living sustainably cannot solely include increased levels of spending and consumerism, but rather a richer vision of the planet that concerns living within our natural environment and basing our economy on its true motor of growth—the natural world, rather than profit, technology, and efficiency.[46]

Studies have shown that increased expenditures per capita in the industrialized world have done very little to increase happiness. In fact, the happiness indicators for the U.K. and the U.S. have declined in the past decade, while GDP expenditures per capita have increased. Ecuadorians refer to the good life as a means of living in a society that values human growth and potential for creativity and integrity. Other scholars refer to this as "bounded capability" in which "people live well within certain clearly defined limits."[47] The normative basis for the Yasuní-ITT proposal is crucial to understanding the political networks and structures that have formed around it. The proposal embodies the larger idea that humans cannot destroy the most pristine areas of the planet without losing part of their own life sustenance. Therefore, Ecuador calls the world to join it in restraining from the drilling of the ITT block of Yasuní as part of the practice of "the good life, or sufficiency, or bounded capabilities." Thus, while some critics of the Yasuní-ITT proposal contend that normative bases of this proposal derive from a small group of indigenous peoples, such assertions neglect the mounting literature from the U.S. and Europe on living within our means *with* nature.

From Alberto Acosta and Eduardo Gudynas's point of view, the neoliberal, market-driven economies of the North have produced "*maldesarrollo,*" or bad development, that cannot be copied by the rest of the world, lest we risk losing nature altogether. For these reasons, Ecuador's new constitution, in various articles,[48] gives rights to nature and calls for an economy based on a market that responds to society's needs, rather than a society built by the market.[49] From the president of Ecuador, Rafael Correa, to leaders inside and outside of the government, those involved in the Yasuní-ITT Initiative contend that the values and norms of the good life from the involvement of indigenous peoples, the protection of the Amazon and other megadiverse areas of the planet, and innovative action against global warming are non-negotiable items on a future global agenda, which Ecuador would like to help lead and develop. As the case of Yasuní-ITT in Ecuador will demonstrate, however, these socio-ecological norms and conceptions of the good life are not without debate and difficulties in translation at national and global levels.

Mapping the Process from Normative Creation
to Initiative and Policy Outcomes

Scholars of transnational advocacy networks have emphasized the dynamics of the network processes from the international level to the domestic level, assuming that international norms will be absorbed by the domestic community or utilized by domestic opposition groups to pressure a repressive regime

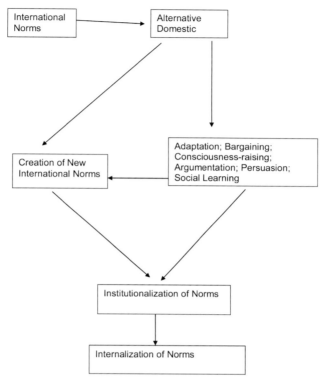

FIGURE 2.1
Dynamic Processes of Global Governance Networks

to change its policies.[50] However, a closer look at the Yasuní-ITT Initiative, aside from its innovative policy implications, points to new directions in network analysis from the South. I attribute this fury of alternative suggestions to a number of causes: 1) the emergence of developing market economies (such as China, Brazil, and India) and their political importance on the international stage; 2) the fallout from the financial crisis and global conversations to rethink post–World War II international institutions and policies; and 3) social learning processes that occurred during the 1990s when many transnational networks formed. As director of International Relations at La Universidad San Francisco de Quito, Ecuador, Carlos Espinosa commented, "This is not the globalization of the 1990s anymore."[51]

The intervening processes of social interaction in the 1990s through many transnational networks, coupled with challenges to Western hegemony and the economic crisis, have created the perfect storm of creative invention in the South. In the first decade of this new century, we have witnessed far more interaction among southern NGOs. Contrary to Clifford Bob's claim of looking for norms that "fit with international agendas," these activists have a clear normative path and have worked with their state to seek international alliances and support, without sacrificing their original desired outcome.[52] Moreover, the leaders of the Yasuní-ITT proposal have searched for normative change within environmental markets, such as the EU ETS, so as to include avoided carbon emissions. Thus, a simple reading of the actors and this proposal might demonstrate just another form of debt-for-nature swap. A closer look, however, reveals the basis of a new type of market logic—one that pays *not* to emit; *not* to extract; and *not* to exploit valuable resources.

Like Checkel, this dynamic process combines the rational bargaining for maximized utility with a serious emphasis on social interaction and learning on domestic and international levels simultaneously.[53] The architects of this proposal within Ecuador and around the world in its various stages of development have disagreed (as we will see) on how to fund avoided oil extraction in the ITT block and how to manage the funds once they are raised. Yet, constant communication among Ecuadorian government leaders and civil society activists locally, nationally, and internationally has resulted in a proposal that reflects the political realities of a country that has had unstable governments and relied on resource extraction for the majority of its public spending, yet seeks a means of integrating its national and international policies and economics in a more sustainable manner.

This reality means that those who simply wanted to offer voluntary citizen contributions on the Internet to finance the project (whom we will examine in the following chapters) had to compromise with those who wanted to preserve oil underground in Yasuní, but felt that some sort of market mechanisms were needed. These discussions, as will be outlined later in the book, were conducted in various forums within Ecuador and around the world. They included people who had lived in Shushufindi in Ecuador's Northern Amazon, which has witnessed incredible amounts of environmental degradation from oil spills, and who are suing Chevron Texaco for them. They also included people who come from international NGO backgrounds that understand the complex bargaining at global levels and the difficulty of pioneering new international norms and structures. Finally, president Rafael Correa, who was elected as a leader of socialism for the twenty-first century has, in the eyes of some of his own supporters, betrayed the pathway to the good life and created roadblocks for the ultimate success of the Yasuní-ITT proposal. He too, as we will see, lives within bounded political realities of government institutions and international financial mechanisms that have been ingrained in the country's development since the 1950s. Thus, negotiation and bargaining have not been solely defined by the current institutions, but the actors have certainly been shaped by their experiences and social relations with one another, which in turn influence the crafting of the proposal and its ultimate success or failure on both national and international levels. Understanding these intricacies is the key not only to saving Yasuní National Park in the Amazon, but also to assisting other megadiverse countries in their quest to live sustainably within their natural environments.

In fact, Tetreault and Lipschutz's model of the "human enterprise" is a significant element in understanding the emergence of this campaign.[54] A simple analysis of NGOs and state interactions would blur the complex and synergistic interactions of those involved in this proposal at all levels. As we witness other alternative proposals to global norms and institutions, such as the United Nations Collaborative Programme on Reducing Emissions from Deforestation and Forest Degradation in Developing Countries (UN-REDD) proposal to expand Kyoto Protocol norms and institutions, this dynamic model may be more applicable to our analysis of global governance networks and their outcomes.

While Risse-Kappen, Ropp, and Sikkink's model for normative socialization processes encapsulates those networks that work within the boomerang effect, this case and others from the South do not fit.[55] In this model, international norms are formed, such as the Kyoto Protocol and its mechanisms of Joint Initiative (JI), Clean Development Mechanism (CDM), and the European Union Emissions Trading Scheme (EU ETS). However, domestic communities, in this case from the South, are not satisfied with these norms and, rather than only countering them with "Battle of Seattle" resistance and protest, they formulate alternative norms and mobilize to institutionalize them. Like the Risse-Kappen et al. model, domestic groups work with the international community (including INGOs, IGOs, other states, and transnational corporations) to create new international norms.[56] This is accomplished through adaptation of their norms to suit the international community and its current structures; bargaining with key players to engage them in dialog and support; consciousness-raising to engage civil society; argumentation and debate over details of norm implementation and institutionalization; persuasion; and social learning. The aspect of social learning is unique to this model, per Checkel's findings.[57] It illustrates the social dimensions of interactions on domestic and international levels, such as the case of leaders for the initiative who have friendships with leaders in other countries and dialog with them about how to best frame the campaign to the international community. This information is then used to restructure characteristics of the initiative on domestic and global levels.

The process of social interaction and norm development began in the mid-1990s. Once enough support for alternative international norms is garnered, actors seek institutionalization at domestic and international levels, as is the case in the Risse-Kappen et al. model. Finally, the new norms become internalized via new institutional mechanisms of global governance structures and, hopefully, replication. The Yasuní-ITT Initiative has received global and domestic support for its alternative norm of "avoided emissions" and protecting uncontacted indigenous peoples. These norms were institutionalized through new governmental structures in Ecuador—namely the Administrative and Leadership Council (CAD) appointed by President Correa in 2008. At the international level, Yasuní-ITT advocates are seeking its institutionalization via monetary support from the international community (including governance of the Ecuador Yasuní-ITT Trust Fund from the United Nations Development Fund) and new agreements on climate change in the post-2012 era.

This model demonstrates that international norms are not always carved in stone; they can change or be altered. It also highlights the significance of viewing international norms from the South, or in this case, from the rainforest. Furthermore, the model underlines the importance of people in the process and their relationships in networks at all levels, and how these relationships influence changes in the institutionalization of norms.

Another aspect of this model that is critical is political opportunity structure (POS).[58] Shifts in norms at all levels require good timing and openness to new concepts. While the creation of new norms does not necessitate POS, the ability to network and persuade others to accept them is dependent upon POS at domestic and global levels. This is the intricacy in trying to change norms and the behaviors that they create at domestic and global levels. The Yasuní-ITT Initiative illustrates the long road of seizing POS during the Correa regime and post-Kyoto discussions on climate change. Although these are structures that have influenced the initiative, the actors involved have surely not been limited by them, as demonstrated by their innovative proposals.

Ironically, in the counter-boomerang effect, domestic actors initiate a campaign *with* the state government. Ultimately, the state becomes the representative of the normative change, institutionalizing it. During the institutionalization phase, the state may distance itself from its original civil society allies, which can cause gaps in knowledge transfer and communication among these actors. During institutionalization and the quest for acceptance at the international level, the state will represent the claim at the global level. In this case, international network collaborators often are privy to information that their domestic counterparts do not have. However, social learning is a critical component of this process. Once the state has institutionalized the norm and interacted at the international level, it then returns to work with domestic civil society to further the initiative. The Yasuní-ITT case will illustrate these dynamics.

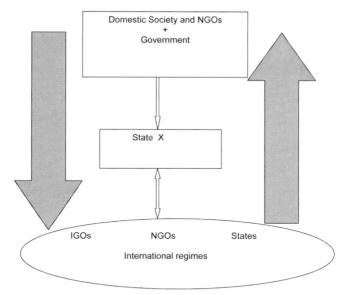

FIGURE 2.2
The Counter-Boomerang Effect

This process may be caused by structural limitations in the international system. As states are often the actors that support and implement new international norms through international organizations and agreements, domestic civil society can be left out of the equation. Here again, social interaction is a key element of this equation. In the case of Yasuní-ITT, domestic supporters who were originally involved in the initiative reengage and ultimately, dialog with the government and international supporters to re-fashion the initiative. Such complex global and local processes underscore the significance of people over structures and social interaction over unidimensional state power approaches.

Methodology

In an effort to best understand social interaction and learning, I conducted structured and unstructured interviews in Ecuador between 2006 and 2009 with an intensive field research period in Ecuador on a Fulbright Scholar Research grant during the spring of 2009. I also observed numerous NGO, oil company, and government meetings during the same time period. The structured interviews were conducted with a series of questions regarding the actor's involvement in the campaign and his normative foundations, as well as his history with the initiative and institutional affiliations. In some cases, I had multiple interviews with an actor, most specifically when the initiative was reformulated, or when new information was available. The translation for the interviews in this book was done by the author with the assistance of a graduate assistant, Andrea Lizarzaburu, to whom I am most grateful.

Additionally, site visits to the park and Waorani indigenous communities provided not only interview opportunities, but also clear observation of the situation in which people live and of the changing environmental dynamics. I have been visiting and studying Ecuador for over thirteen years, in which time I have seen dramatic changes to Yasuní National Park and the surrounding communities. This "groundwork" is a means of verifying the scientific data on environmental impacts, oil spills, and social changes that they document.

Finally, the institutional information and actor agency is further documented via news, media, and government reports and official documents. This method provides another optic of the networks and their normative foundations. Such analysis is significant as much of the normative development of this initiative is documented in scholarly studies and the Ecuadorian constitution passed in 2008.

While researcher perspective is always an issue in qualitative analysis, I have sought to disengage myself from active participation in the initiative, although I clearly wish it success. The people involved in this initiative have provided me with incomparable perspective on the good life and how it can be applied to global politics. They have spent endless hours explaining this process to me and have invited me into their homes and their lives. Any error in this examination is mine alone, and any criticism of the process is meant as a policy analysis. In sum, the actors involved in this initiative are a testament not just to what human enterprise can do in the present, but to what its possibilities are in the future.

Notes

1. Matthias Finger, "Which Governance for Sustainable Development? An Organizational and Institutional Perspective," in *The Crisis of Global Environmental Governance: Towards a New Political Economy of Sustainability*, ed. Jacob Park, Ken Conca, and Matthias Finder (New York: Routledge, 2008), 34.

2. Stephen D. Krasner, "Structural Causes and Regime Consequences: Regimes as Intervening Variables," in *International Regimes* (Ithaca, NY: Cornell University Press, 1982); Martin Wolf, "Will the Nation State Survive Globalization?" *Foreign Affairs* 80, no. 1 (February 2001): 178–190.

3. Anthony Giddens, *Runaway World: How Globalization Is Reshaping Our Lives* (New York: Routledge, 2000); Barry K. Gills, *Globalization and Global History. Lon-*

don (New York: Routledge, 2005); David Held and Anthony McGrew, *Globalization/ Anti-Globalization* (Oxford: Polity, 2002); Leslie F. Sklair, *Globalization, Capitalism, and Its Alternatives* (Oxford: Oxford University Press, 2002); Jan Aart Scholte, "Civil Society and Democracy in Global Governance," *Global Governance* 8, no. 3 (July–Sept 2002): 281–306.

4. Thomas D. Hall and Christopher Chase-Dunn, "Global Social Change in the Long Run," in *Global Social Change: Historical and Comparative Perspectives*, ed. Christopher Chase-Dunn and Salvatore Babones (Baltimore, MD: Johns Hopkins University Press, 2006), 33–58.

5. Guillaume Fontaine, *El Precio del Petróleo* (Quito, Ecuador: Abya Yala, 2007); Eduardo Gudynas, *Ecología, Economía y Ética del Desarrollo Sostenible* (Quito, Ecuador: Abya Yala, 2003); Pablo Ortiz T., *Globalización y Conflictos Socioambientales* (Quito, Ecuador: Abya Yala, 1997).

6. Alberto Acosta, *Desarrollo Glocal: Con la Amazonía en la Mira* (Quito, Ecuador: Corporación Editora Nacional, 2005).

7. Alberto Acosta, interview with author, Quito, Ecuador, February 27, 2009.

8. Ken Conca, *Governing Water: Contentious Transnational Politics and Global Institution Building* (Cambridge, MA: MIT Press, 2006), 45.

9. From James N. Rosenau, *Distant Proximities: Dynamics beyond Globalization* (Princeton, NJ: Princeton University Press, 2003).

10. Sklair, *Globalization.*

11. Allison Brysk, *From Tribal Village to Global Village: Indian Rights and International Relations in Latin America* (Stanford, CA: Stanford University Press, 2000); Margaret E. Keck and Kathryn Sikkink, *Activists beyond Borders: Advocacy Networks in International Politics* (Ithaca, NY: Cornell University Press, 1998); Pamela L. Martin, *The Globalization of Contentious Politics: The Amazonian Indigenous Rights Movement* (New York: Routledge, 2003); Pamela L. Martin and Franke Wilmer, "Transnational Normative Struggles and Globalization: The Case of Indigenous Peoples in Bolivia and Ecuador," *Globalizations* 5, no. 4 (December 2008): 583–598.

12. Jeffrey T. Checkel, "Why Comply? Social Learning and European Identity Change," *International Organization* 55, no. 3 (Summer 2001): 553–588.

13. Liliana B. Andonova, Michele M. Betsill, and Harriet Bulkeley, "Transnational Climate Governance," *Global Environmental Politics* 9, no. 2, 52–73.

14. Robert O'Brien, Anne Marie Goetz, Jan Aart Scholte, and Marc Williams, *Contesting Global Governance: Multilateral Economic Institutions and Global Social Movements* (Cambridge, Cambridge University Press, 2006); Mary Ann Tetreault and Ronnie D. Lipschutz, *Global Politics as if People Mattered* (Lanham, MD: Rowman and Littlefield, 2005); Conca, *Governing Water*; Ronnie D. Lipschutz and Judith Mayer, *Global Civil Society and Global Environmental Governance: The Politics of Nature from Place to Planet* (Albany, NY: State University of New York, 1996).

15. Krasner, "Structural Causes."

16. Tetreault and Lipschutz, *Global Politics.*

17. Kathryn Hochstetler and Margaret E. Keck, *Greening Brazil* (Durham, NC: Duke University Press, 2007), 3.

18. Sidney Tarrow, *The New Transnational Activism* (Cambridge: Cambridge University Press, 2005).

19. James N. Rosenau, *Along the Domestic-Foreign Frontier: Exploring Governance in a Turbulent World* (Cambridge: Cambridge University Press, 1997).

20. Andonova, Betsill, and Bulkeley's "Transnational Climate Governance" outlines such differences as well.

21. I refer to the typology of transnational climate change governance networks and their functions here by Andonova et al. (ibid.).

22. Input and output sides of legitimacy are also discussed in Eva Lövbrand, Teresia Rindefjäll, and Joakim Nordqvist, "Closing the Legitimacy Gap in Global Environmental Governance?" *Global Environmental Politics* 9, no. 2 (May 2009): 74–100.

23. James N. Rosenau, *People Count! Networked Individuals in Global Politics* (Boulder, CO: Paradigm Publishers, 2008).

24. Conca, *Governing Water*, 59.

25. Some scholars have noted that movements across borders, or "transnational movements," have arisen as a response to increased networks in a globalized society. Their findings conclude that while few movements are completely global in identity and action, many utilize new technology, travel, and communication resources to create change on both local and global levels. See Robert O. Keohane and Joseph S. Nye, *Transnational Relations and World Politics* (Cambridge, MA: MIT Press, 1971); Keck and Sikkink, *Activists beyond Borders*; Brysk, *From Tribal Village*; Tarrow, *New Transnational Activism*; Joe Bandy and Jackie Smith, eds., *Coalitions across Borders: Transnational Protest and the Neoliberal Order* (Lanham, MD: Rowman and Littlefield, 2005); Leslie J. Wood, "Bridging the Chasms: The Case of Peoples' Global Action," in *Coalitions across Borders: Transnational Protest and the Neoliberal Order*, edited by Joe Bandy and Jackie Smith (Lanham, MD: Rowman and Littlefield, 2005), 95–120.

26. Sanjeev Khagram and Saleem H. Ali, "Transnational Transformations: From Government-centric Interstate Regimes to Cross-sectoral Multi-level Networks of Global Governance," in *The Crisis of Global Governance: Toward a New Political Economy of Sustainability*, ed. Jacob Park, Ken Conca, and Matthias Finger (New York: Routledge, 2008), 158–159.

27. Chukwumerije Okereke and Harriet Buklekey, "Conceptualizing Climate Change Governance beyond the International Regime: A Review of Four Theoretical Approaches," Tyndall Centre for Climate Change Research, http://www.tyndall.ac.uk/publications/working_papers/twp112.pdf., 69.

28. Esperanza Martínez, "De Kyoto a Quito," *Llacta! Acción Ecológica*, May 9, 2007, http://www.llacta.org/organiz/coms/2007/com0096.htm.

29. Alexander E. Wendt, "The Agent-Structure Problem in International Relations Theory," *International Organization* 41, no. 3 (1987): 236–370; Keck and Sikkink, *Activists beyond Borders*; Sanjeev Khagram, James Riker, and Kathryn Sikkink, eds., *Restructuring World Politics: Transnational Social Movements, Networks and Norms* (Minneapolis: University of Minnesota Press, 2002); Martha Finnemore, "Norms, Culture and World Politics: Insights from Sociology's Institutionalism," *International Organization* 50, no. 2 (Spring 1996): 325–347.

30. Keck and Sikkink, *Activists beyond Borders*; William E. DeMars, *NGOs and Transnational Networks: Wild Cards in World Politics* (London: Pluto Press, 2005); Paul Wapner, *Environmental Activism and World Civic Politics* (Albany: State University of New York, 1996).

31. Hochstetler and Keck discuss the Brazilian socio-environmental movement and describe it as "an attempt to make compatible the struggles for environmental sustainability and for sustainable livelihoods. Opposed to a purely expansionist capitalism on social and ecological grounds, it argues that empowering poor people *and* responding to their demands for social equity must be an integral part of any solution to environmental problems" (*Greening Brazil*, 13). Many Ecuadorian environmental NGOs and actors subscribe to these norms as well.

32. Alberto Acosta, "El Buen Vivir, una oportunidad por construir," *Portal de Economía Solidaria*, February 17, 2009 (translation by Pamela L. Martin).

33. Gudynas, *Ecología, Economía y Ética.*

34. Gudynas, *Ecología, Economía y Ética*, 162.

35. Herman Daly, review of section 1, chapter 1 of Agenda 21 (International Policies to Accelerate Sustainable Development in Developing Countries and Related Domestic Policies), *Population and Environment* 15, no. 1 (September 1993): 66–69.

36. James Gustave Speth, *The Bridge at the Edge of the World* (New Haven, CT: Yale University Press, 2008).

37. Bill McKibben, *Deep Economy: The Wealth of Communities and the Future* (New York: Times Books, 2007).

38. Paul Hawken, *Blessed Unrest: How the Largest Social Movement in History Is Restoring Grace, Justice, and Beauty to the World* (New York: Penguin, 2007).

39. Acosta, "El Buen Vivir"; Gudynas, *Ecología, Economía y Ética.*

40. Joseph E. Aldy and Robert N. Stavins, *Post-Kyoto International Climate Policy: Summary for Policymakers* (Cambridge: Cambridge University Press, 2009).

41. Paul J. Nelson and Ellen Dorsey, *New Rights Advocacy: Changing Strategies of Development and Human Rights NGOs* (Washington, D.C.: Georgetown University Press, 2008).

42. Ibid.

43. Thomas Princen, *The Logic of Sufficiency* (Cambridge, MA: MIT Press, 2005); Thomas Princen, Michael Maniates, and Ken Conca, eds., *Confronting Consumption* (Cambridge, MA: MIT Publishers, 2000).

44. Princen, *Logic of Sufficiency.*

45. Ibid., 18.

46. Alberto Acosta, "El petróleo en el Ecuador: Una evaluación crítica del pasado cuarto del siglo," in *El Ecuador Post Petrolero* (Quito, Ecuador: Acción Ecológica, Idlis, and Oilwatch, 2000), 3–33.

47. Tim Jackson, *Prosperity without Growth: The Transition to a Sustainable Economy* (London: Sustainable Development Commission, 2010), 34–35.

48. Articles 15, 57, 72, 73, 281, 395, 313, 317, 397, 407, 413, 417 in the 2008 constitution.

49. Acosta, "El Buen Vivir."

50. Thomas Risse-Kappen, Stephen C. Ropp, and Kathryn Sikkink, *The Power of Human Rights: International Norms and Domestic Change* (Cambridge: Cambridge University Press, 1999); Keck and Sikkink, *Activists beyond Borders*; Tarrow, *New Transnational Activism.*

51. Personal communication to author, Quito, Ecuador, March 2009.

52. Clifford Bob, *The Marketing of Rebellion: Insurgents, Media, and International Activism* (Cambridge: Cambridge University Press, 2005).

53. Checkel, "Why Comply?" 553–588.

54. Tetreault and Lipschutz, *Global Politics.*

55. Risse-Kappen, Ropp, and Sikkink, *Power of Human Rights.*

56. Ibid.

57. Checkel, "Why Comply?" 553–588.

58. Charles Tilly, *From Mobilization to Revolution* (New York: McGraw Hill Publishing, 1978).

3

History in Black, Green, and Red

F ORMER MINISTER OF foreign affairs and personal representative to President Correa for the Yasuní-ITT Initiative, Francisco Carrión Mena calls it *ilusionante* (thrilling). What is so thrilling about this part of the world is its biodiversity, not just compared to other places on the planet, but even compared to other places in the Amazon. ITT stands for Ishpingo-Tambococha-Tiputini. It is one block (also known as Block 43) within the Yasuní Man and the Biosphere Reserve under the UNESCO Man and the Biosphere program, which comprises Yasuní National Park and the Waorani Ethnic Reserve. While the Yasuní-ITT Initiative and the campaign surrounding it refer specifically to saving this one extremely biodiverse block within the park, supporters aspire to protect the entire park by demonstrating the significance of this project to global climate change initiatives.

The other part of the Yasuní-ITT story that is *ilusionante* is that it sits on one of Ecuador's largest oil reserves and is where two communities of uncontacted indigenous peoples live. Thus, saving the ITT block and the greater park includes more than just keeping oil underground and biodiversity safe for our planet; it also protects the fundamental human right of self-determination. This chapter will examine the interconnected histories of oil extraction, indigenous rights, and the governance of Yasuní National Park, ending in an explanation of how the proposal to leave oil underground in this area was conceived and how it developed into an international proposal.

Yasuní National Park and Its People

The history of the park is rife with global governance networks. The Yasuní National Park was created in 1979 with 678,000 hectares, but its limits were reduced to 544,730 hectares in 1990 to avoid lawsuit over international oil concession bids within the park.[1] However in May 1992, its area was expanded to 982,000 hectares.[2] According to ecologist Dr. Matt Finer and his colleagues, this area is within the "core Amazon," a particularly wet section that researchers expect will remain wet, even as "climate change–induced drought intensifies in the eastern Amazon over the coming decades."[3]

The extreme levels of biodiversity of this park have been noted by various scholars, including a group of fifty-nine scientists concerned for Yasuní, who wrote a letter to then-Ecuadorian President Gutierrez, pleading with him to reject oil development that would allow road construction.[4] Other scientists who work out of the two university-affiliated research stations have found that the park, beyond being one of the least deforested areas of the Amazon, is home to the highest documented number of amphibians and reptiles (150 and 121 species, respectively), over 600 avian species (also one of the world's record-holders), and the highest concentration in a small area of tree species of all places on the planet—more than in all of North America combined. Many endangered species—vertebrate, mammal, and plant—can be found in this park, including two globally endangered mammals: the white-bellied spider monkey and the giant otter.[5] Dr. Finer calls these attributes "the trifecta." "The Yasuní region is the 1) most biodiverse, 2) most intact, and 3) wettest section of the Amazon Basin, making it one of the premier conservation sites in the world." He says, "Quite simply, Yasuní National Park and the surrounding intact forest of the northwest Amazon is one of the last best hopes for sustaining Amazonian biodiversity and wilderness in the long term."[6]

In addition to its natural biodiversity, this area is home to several uncontacted indigenous Waorani communities (primarily Tagaeri, Taromenane, and possibly, Oñamenane peoples) who have a history of resisting outside influence. While the population estimates vary in the hundreds for these *intangibles* (uncontacted), the contacted Waorani communities are estimated at nearly 3,000 people in total, comprising thirty-eight Waorani communities with a growth rate of 2.2–2.5 percent per year.[7] The history of this group has been controversial, and the Waorani have used violence against missionaries, illegal timber loggers, and oil company workers. While more is known about the Tagaeri, who have been associated with the killing of oil company workers in the 1970s and the Capuchin missionary Alejandro Labaka, the Taromenane are less understood.[8]

In January 2009, a mother and her three children were walking on a new road being built near where researchers suspect Taromenane and Tagaeri populations live. Sandra Zabala, the mother, and her two children were found slain on that road with spears identified as those made by Taromenane and Tagaeri. Her six-month-old baby was found miraculously alive three days later deep in the jungle. The slayings occurred in the Los Reyes area of the Francisco de Orellana province, ten kilometers from the delineation of the *zona intangible* (uncontacted zone, ZI). Such violence has brought these uncontacted groups to the forefront again as locals and researchers argue that the slayings are a sign to stay away from their areas. Researchers suspect that the killing was carried out by Taromenane, a group that the Waorani say went deeper into the forest to avoid contact with others.[9] Evidence of these uncontacted communities also has been found in parts of oil blocks located in the park, including numbers 14, 16, 17, and 31.[10]

Like Yasuní National Park, the *zona intangible* (ZI) is embedded within the structures and processes of global governance. In 1997, a report to the Inter-American Commission on Human Rights (IACHR) recognized the rights of uncontacted Tagaeri and Taromenane peoples. The Ecuadorian government responded by creating the ZI within the park to protect them in January 1999, which made logging and oil operations illegal in this area.[11] In the interim, more illegal loggers used the Auca road, built for oil operations in the 1980s, to move deeper into the ZI.

In May 2003, nine Waorani men killed twelve Taromenane, mostly women and children, within the ZI. Some researchers speculate that this was a revenge killing and others speculate it was to gain deeper access in the forest for logging; still others report that up to thirty people died in this attack.[12] In April 2006, the Taromenane speared two loggers who were in their territory, which spawned unconfirmed reports of revenge killings by the loggers in the ZI. In response to this violence, a group of activists concerned for those living in voluntary isolation took the case to the IACHR to pressure the Ecuadorian government to implement strong standards against entry into the park. In May 2006, the IACHR ruled that precautionary measures should be in place in the ZI. In January 2007, then-president Alfredo Palacio decreed the final ZI of 7,580 square kilometers, which includes the southern half of the park and parts of the Waorani Ethnic Reserve, and five oil blocks.[13] The southern part of the ITT block is included in the ZI.

Park Governance?

Given Yasuní National Park's extreme biodiversity and indigenous population—contacted groups and those living in voluntary isolation—in addition to the fact that it is the country's only Amazonian national park, one would expect significant funding to protect it. Yet of all national parks in the country, it receives the least monetary support and has the smallest technical staff to administrate it. Of the estimated $348,434 to $699,681 needed to protect the park, it received only $88,130 in 2007.[14] Anthropologists Guillaume Fontaine and Ivan Narváez argue that the governability of Yasuní National Park is on the border of collapse, unless new global governance structures are implemented quickly. They note that Yasuní is already part of international environmental regimes, such as the Stockholm Declaration of 1972, the Earth Charter of 1982, the Brundtland Report of 1987, the Rio Declaration and Agenda 21 of 1992, and the Millennium Declaration of 2000.[15] The application for the park to be a UNESCO Man and Biosphere Reserve was devised and presented to UNESCO by an international NGO, The Nature Conservancy (TNC), and the director of natural areas of the sub-secretariat of forest and natural resources of Ecuador. Fontaine contends that local populations were not consulted on this and even environmental groups were opposed to the designation because they felt it communicated a tacit approval of oil companies within the biosphere.[16]

The park's governance is an amalgam of actors with no clear hierarchy; although the Ministry of Energy and Mines seems to claim a higher level of authority than other actors. It includes a board of directors, composed of local governmental, non-governmental, and indigenous organizations, plus scientists from the two university research stations in the park. The Ministry of the Environment has also created a technical advisory board with members from the National Environmental Fund, the Ministry of the Environment, and researchers from the two research stations, plus the Center for Tropical Forest Research. Additionally, the Ministry of the Environment and the National Direction of Environmental Protection (DINAPA—the environmental enforcement institution of the Ministry of Energy and Mines) have legal authority within park governance. Finally, oil companies have direct interaction with these advisory and governance institutions as they present their environmental impact assessments (EIAs) to them and, ultimately, seek licensing for the blocks in the park.[17]

Ricardo Crespo Plaza argues that the governance mechanisms for the park are weak and decentralized, which allows DINAPA primary authority in oil concessions within the park. Ivan Narváez sums up the governance model of the park as "the extractivist model of petroleum exploitation implemented by a State that is conditioned by economics, politically exclusive, socially unequal, and ethically questionable."[18] Weaving through these governance structures are municipal governments that often work directly with oil companies and support their concessions, even within the park, as a means of local revenue.[19] In various interviews in Quito and Coca, oil company leaders and government representatives noted their mutual collaboration.[20] Thus, the global governance networks include private and public actors at multiple levels in the international system.

Black Gold and the Resource Curse

Nearly half of Ecuador's territory is Amazonian, covering 130,000 square kilometers, or 2 percent of the entire Amazonian region in South America. Five percent of the country's population lives in the area, which has experienced rapid growth from 263,797 people in 1982 to 372,563 in 1990 and then to 613,339 people in 2000.[21] While the Ecuadorian government encouraged colonization of the Amazon throughout the 1960s and 1970s, as did other countries of the basin, prosperity has not favored colonists. Instead, they rank among the poorest members of their society. While 54.5% of Ecuadorians from the Highlands, or Sierra, rank among the poor, 79.2 % of their Amazonian neighbors are classified as poor, according to Ecuador's National Institute of Statistics.[22] The percentage of people living in poverty in the provinces most impacted by oil development is even higher: 82.4% in Sucumbíos and 80.2% in Orellana. Additionally, literacy rates are far lower in this part of the country and clean drinking water is provided to only 13% and 14% of the population of this area (in Sucumbíos and Orellana, respectively), as compared to the national average of 48%.[23]

In terms of oil reserves, Ecuador ranks fourth in Latin America, having thirty-two petroleum blocks with approximately 5.6 billion barrels of oil. It is number eleven on the list of countries that export oil to the United States, down from number six only two years ago—due in large part to conflicts with US oil companies and state licensing agreements, plus decreased production.[24] Oil production is 43 percent of the country's exports and has been the principal source of state income since 1973. The ITT block is estimated to have 846 million barrels of recoverable petroleum, which is heavy crude—about 14.7 API.[25] The daily production of oil is estimated at approximately 107,000 barrels for thirteen years, with a continual declining production for twelve more years. Independent reports conducted for Petroproducción Ecuador indicate that proven reserves are 944 million barrels of heavy crude and that there may be up to another 1,530 billion barrels of reserves.[26]

Engineer Mauro Dávila of Petroproducción Ecuador was directly involved in the evaluations of the block and contends that there is more oil to the western edge of this area, based on evaluation of crude oil reserves that began in 1997. The 2004 report and one that was conducted in 2008 include two more oil

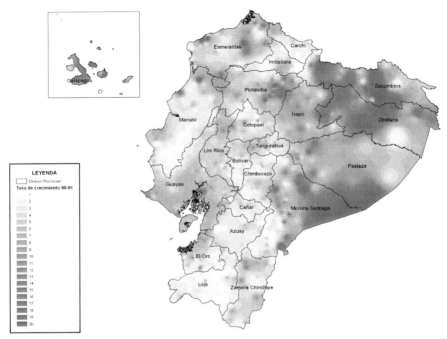

MAP 3.1
Ecuador Population Growth
Source: INEC, *Censos de Población y Vivienda*, 1974, 1982, 1990, 2001, from Carlos Larrea, Ana Isabel
Larrea, and Ana Lucia Bravo, "*Petróleo, sustentabilidad y desarrollo en la Amazonía ecuatoriana: Dilemas
para una transición hacia una sociedad post-petrolera*, 2008, unpublished manuscript.

fields, Ishpingo 3 and Ishpingo 4. The total findings of crude oil are about 21–22
percent of Ecuador's proven reserves. According to Dávila, a petroleum engineer for the state company, the Yasuní proposal is worthy of support. He says:

> As you can see Ecuador is also suffering an economic downturn as a result of the
> global economic crisis; therefore, we need money and crude oil is a substantial
> source of money for the country. If a government launches an idea of conserv-
> ing the environment, it is praiseworthy although unusual, because people would
> tend to put environmentalists, green concepts aside and go for the money. If you
> analyze and consider why Ecuador wants to give up the riches underground to
> preserve the environment, it is actually interesting because crude oil is there and
> the possibility is that there is even more.[27]

Of course, part of the history of the Yasuní-ITT Initiative is the criticism
that the government is competing with itself, on one hand, to launch a campaign to leave oil underground, and on the other hand, to research reserves
in this block and prepare for bidding concessions with the state company

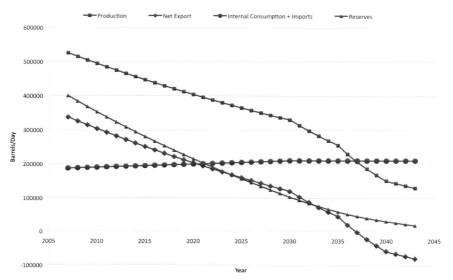

FIGURE 3.1
Petroleum Projections in Ecuador: 2007–2042 (Barrels per Year)
Source: Banco central del Ecuador, 2007 (www.bce.fin.ec), from Carlos Larrea, Ana Isabel Larrea, and Ana
Lucia Bravo, "Petróleo, sustentabilidad y desarrollo en la Amazonía ecuatoriana: Dilemas para una tran-
sición hacia una sociedad post-petrolera, 2008, unpublished manuscript.

Petroecuador. Petroproducción, a state company that is dedicated to oil exploration and the operation of hydrocarbon activities of the country, has officially supported the initiative. In fact, Dávila, who has spent an entire career
drilling oil in the Amazon, says:

> Thus, we have enough information. The objective is to be prepared in case the
> Yasuní Initiative ends up not working out, which would be a shame because it is
> a beautiful zone. But, we have to be prepared to carry out operations in the best
> possible ways. The idea is to minimize the risk; there is no hundred-percent-safe
> operation. There will not be a guarantee that no accidents could occur during
> practice. Nevertheless, we will try to keep them to the minimum; and that is why
> we have everything ready.[28]

During the interview, Dávila said that new seismic testing was strongly supported by the state government in other parts of the Amazon, most specifically those bordering Peru, as demonstrated in maps 3.2 and 3.3. Thus, while
the initiative to save Yasuní has a chance to be successful, it is still not clear
what the outcome would be for the rest of the Amazonian region. He also was
not aware of any funding toward alternative energy production from the state
government.[29] These new modes of energy for the country are supposed to be
funded by the income from the Yasuní-ITT Initiative.

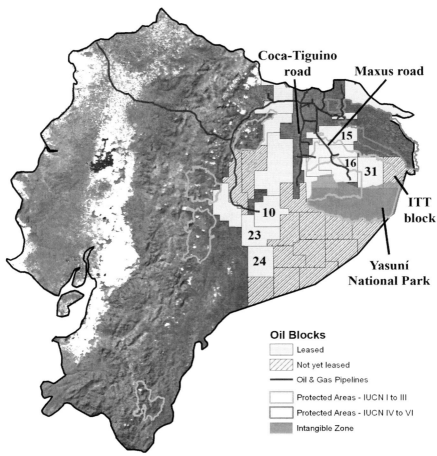

Oil Blocks

- Leased
- Not yet leased
- Oil & Gas Pipelines
- Protected Areas - IUCN I to III
- Protected Areas - IUCN IV to VI
- Intangible Zone

MAP 3.2
Ecuador Oil Blocks

Source: M. Finer, C. N. Jenkins, S. L. Pimm, B. Keane, and C. Ross, "Oil and Gas Projects in the Western Amazon: Threats to Wilderness, Biodiversity, and Indigenous Peoples," *PLoS ONE* 3, no. 8 (2008): e2932. doi:10.1371/journal.pone.0002932.

A History of the Initiative

The ITT international campaign is a stellar example of how to protect rare and biodiverse areas on our planet and it dovetails with the United Nations Intergovernmental Panel on Climate Change (IPCC) 2007 report, which calls on policy makers worldwide to decrease the use of petroleum while increasing and preserving forests.[30] It also comes on the heels of an internationally well-known lawsuit filed against Chevron Texaco (formerly

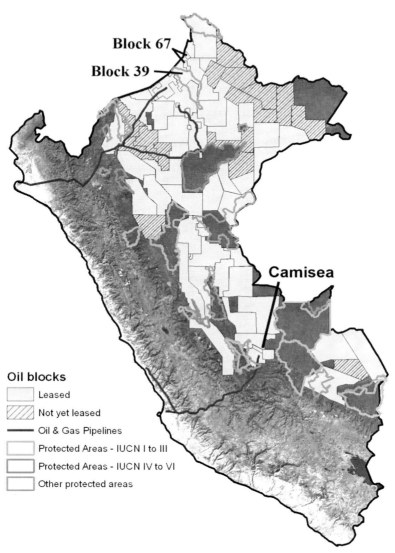

Oil blocks

- Leased
- Not yet leased
- Oil & Gas Pipelines
- Protected Areas - IUCN I to III
- Protected Areas - IUCN IV to VI
- Other protected areas

Block 67

Block 39

Camisea

MAP 3.3
Peru Oil Blocks

Source: M. Finer, C. N. Jenkins, S. L. Pimm, B. Keane, and C. Ross, "Oil and Gas Projects in the Western Amazon: Threats to Wilderness, Biodiversity, and Indigenous Peoples," *PLoS ONE* 3, no. 8 (2008): e2932. doi:10.1371/journal.pone.0002932.

PHOTO 3.1
An example of environmental destruction in the Lago Agrio area.

Texaco) beginning in 1993 in New York City and culminating in a small courtroom in Lago Agrio, Ecuador, (which ironically means "Sour Lake" in English) in 2008. The case was deemed the "David and Goliath" of its time and was filed on behalf of over 30,000 indigenous and *colono* peoples who claim that the company destroyed the ecology of their northern Amazonian province and left behind grave social and health problems, including high cancer rates.[31] The case is still pending and has taken a number of twists and turns from accusations of fraud on both sides to corruption.

Learning from the Past

International and local Ecuadorian NGOs, including Oilwatch, Amazon Watch, Rainforest Action Network (RAN), Pachamama Alliance, Acción Ecológica, and Frente de Defensa de la Amazonía, have been protesting the inadequacy of Texaco's alleged cleanup and calling for compensation. Writing in her book *Amazon Crude*, Judith Kimerling claims that the oil spill is larger than that of the Exxon Valdez in Alaska.[32] But the "Yasuní Park Depends on You" International Campaign (the original name of the campaign sponsored by Acción Ecológica with other INGOS) is different, as Esperanza Martínez of Acción Ecológica argues, because the world community now knows of the destruction of the rainforest and the devastating impacts that oil extraction and industry can bring not just to plant and animal life, but to the daily lives of indigenous peoples.[33]

Learning from the previous campaign surrounding the Chevron Texaco case and others in the southern Amazon, such as Sarayacu, activists, researchers, and scholars began calling for a moratorium on oil drilling in this region in the mid-1990s. In 2000, Alberto Acosta and Acción Ecológica published a book entitled *El Ecuador Post Petrolero*, which called for a moratorium on oil extraction in the Amazon and a move toward alternative energy sources for the country.[34] This laid the groundwork for a larger plan that included opposition to global climate change, support for those portions of the developing world not included in the Kyoto Protocol, and protection for the rainforest and for those uncontacted peoples living within it.

In October 2006, the international NGO Oilwatch and Acción Ecológica jointly sponsored a forum on human rights, oil, and reparation in the Amazonian town of Coca. The forum hosted leaders and people from all over the world in the rainforest to take a toxi-tour of its devastation and exchange their problems, strategies, and hopes for a better future. It also celebrated ten years of Oilwatch's international mobilization on behalf of rainforests in the southern hemisphere. The forum began with a tour of contaminated sites in the Amazon, followed by a march for human rights and the dignity of the peoples who live in affected areas. It culminated in an exchange of experiences from peoples all over the global South. This event was a key element in discussing alternatives to petroleum extraction and fostering information sharing between leaders in similar situations around the globe.

Gaining Momentum and Political Opportunity

The forum roughly coincided with the presidential election of Rafael Correa, who began his term in January 2007. His election was significant, as the newly formed cabinet and supporters were members of the anti–oil extraction community. Furthermore, his first minister of foreign affairs, María Fernanda Espinosa Garcés, was formerly the International Union for Conservation of Nature (IUCN) regional director for South America and senior advisor on biodiversity and indigenous peoples. When President Correa announced his official support of leaving oil underground in the ITT block in June 2007, he designated the study of the proposal to the Ministry of Foreign Affairs, headed by Minister Espinosa.

According to former minister of energy and mines, Alberto Acosta, the first phase of strategizing about an official proposal began in January 2007, after President Correa's election. Before becoming minister, Acosta worked with Acción Ecológica leader, Esperanza Martínez, on a plan for leaving oil underground. Once he was appointed minister, Acosta worked with Martínez to refine the proposal for its eventual presentation to President Correa. Acosta remembers the time period between January and June 2007 as one of tension between the ministry and the executive president of Petroecuador, Carlos Pareja Yannuzzelli. This illustrates the push and pull between governmental institutions involved in this process. While Acosta supported the proposal to leave oil underground, Pareja sought outside contracts from La Industria Petrolera de Venezuela (PdVsa), Sinopec of China, Petrobras of Brazil, and Enap of Chile in an attempt to convince the president to drill for oil. However, during the Petroecuador board meeting on March 30, 2007, President Correa accepted the proposal to leave oil underground.[35]

On June 5, 2007, President Correa officially announced his support of the Yasuní-ITT proposal, but with the caveat that the international community had to compensate Ecuador for its sacrifice of 20 percent of its reserves. He stated, "Ecuador doesn't ask for charity, but does ask that the international community shares in the sacrifice and compensates us with at least half of what our country would receive, in recognition of the environmental benefits that would be generated by keeping this oil underground."[36] The proposal immediately caught international attention and by later that June, Amazon Watch, a San Francisco–based NGO, sponsored high-publicity trips by Hollywood's Darryl Hannah and Q'Orianka Kilcher to visit the affected areas. Trudie Styler, Sting's wife and founder of the Rainforest Foundation, also visited Yasuní and pledged her support with clips of the campaign and the park in Sting's concerts. Footage of Yasuní narrated by Martin Sheen was even played during the July 7, 2007, Live Earth concert series, organized by former United States vice president Al Gore. By 2010, the theme of the movie *Avatar* was being compared to the campaign to save Yasuní National Park; there was even a premier showing of the movie for indigenous leaders in Quito, Ecuador.[37]

Yet even the celebrity status of the proposal could not disguise the fact that President Correa had accepted it with a Plan A (leaving oil underground) and a Plan B (extracting oil). Thus, as oil prices soared in the summer of 2007, President Correa announced an agreement for the possible contracting of the ITT block with Enap, Sinopec, and Petrobras. From this moment, the Yasuní-ITT Initiative would begin its zigzag policy approach, swaying between Plans A and B.[38]

However, the proposal gained international momentum and support when, on September 24, 2007, President Correa presented it before the United Nations at a meeting on global climate change. He said, "For the first time in history, an oil producing country—dependent on oil export for one third of its budget—proposes to forgo this income for the well-being of humanity . . . [Ecuador] invites the world to join our effort through fair compensation in order to lay the foundations for a more humane and fair civilization."[39] Following the address, the president presented the plan at the Clinton Global Initiative in New York City. The plan was awarded an honorable mention.

Behind the scenes of these public events, transnational networks and national institutional arrangements were emerging. According to Max Christian, formerly of the Sustainable Development and Conservation Biology program at the University of Maryland and former member of a US working group on the ITT block, President Correa had worked with ambassador Luís Gallegos and Organization of American States (OAS) representative Gustavo Palacio in Washington, D.C., to ask international experts to study the options for revenue-substitution for the ITT project to finance the moratorium on Yasuní, effectively seeking governance options outside the sovereign state. In addition, the Wallace Global Fund (in conjunction with the Clinton Global Initiative) funded a World Resources Institute (WRI) study of the viability of revenue substitution models, such as carbon trading and debt cancellation. As Christian pointed out, "these models have implications on a global scale and they may provide new options for avoided carbon emissions from leaving oil in place in order to protect biodiversity and indigenous cultures, not a currently accepted methodology by the United Nations Framework Convention on Climate Change."[40] In order to protect biodiversity and indigenous cultures, researchers at this point in the initiative were looking to interject the idea of leaving the oil unexploited into the post-Kyoto framework discussions that were gearing up to take place in Bali in December 2007.[41]

The Transnational Networks that Bridge North and South

A web sphere analysis of the two most prominent websites for the campaign and their links in the initial stage of development of the proposal in 2007 reveals that southern-based NGOs are not explicitly listed on the website Live Yasuní that was created by Amazon Watch, Save America's Forests, Finding Species, and Max Christian, all NGOs and actors based in the United States.[42] Given the prevalence of Internet use for coordination and website construction in this campaign, an examination of the sites that are officially linked to the main websites indicates network partners and the closeness of their affiliation. In table 3.1, the bold actors are ones that are common in both of the main websites, and all are US-based NGOs. While Amazonía por la Vida is linked to the Live Yasuní website, its Ecuadorian and southern-based NGO partners are not so linked, as illustrated in the

TABLE 3.1
Yasuní-ITT Websites and Linked Actors

Live Yasuní	*Amazonía por la Vida (Amazon for Life)*
Amazonía por la Vida	**Live Yasuní**
WRI	**Amazon Watch**
Earth Economics	**Save America's Forests**
Save America's Forests	**Finding Species**
Finding Species	Amazon Def. Coalition
Amazon Watch	The Pachamama Alliance
Land Is Life	Centro de Derechos Económicos
Wallace Global Fund	Oilwatch
U of MD	Acción Ecológica

right-hand column. Therefore, the Live Yasuní website (developed around the Live Earth concert series of 2007) did not directly incorporate Ecuadorian and southern-based partners. Such analysis illustrates the distances and challenges of organizing in global civil society.

Mitch Anderson from Amazon Watch admitted that some southern-based organizations were skeptical of the need for a website other than the Amazonía por la Vida. While he did specify that there was communication from both southern and northern NGOs over the two-week period that it took to develop the site, he also stated that there were tensions among southern and northern partners. Anderson related, "more communication between the two during this time period would have been helpful."[43]

Interestingly, the sticking point of the Live Yasuní website (which had the potential to expose the campaign to over 2 billion viewers of the Live Earth concert) was whether this site would act as the recipient of monetary pledges to the campaign to pay for keeping oil underground in the park. Such a payment scheme has not developed as of yet, which some activists found (and still find) frustrating. Instead, Live Yasuní allows viewers to sign a petition of support for the campaign. The joint Skype voice-over-Internet-protocol (VOIP) and telephone conversations about the development of Live Yasuní established that it would act as a portal to direct supporters to the Amazonía por la Vida website and to eventually establish a system of supporter payment on the Amazonía por la Vida site. The analysis of this web sphere information reveals that while northern and southern NGOs collaborated on this campaign, 1) much of the fanfare and publicity had been directed toward northern NGOs, 2) the technical support from the North created the Live Yasuní campaign, which expanded its audience and potential support, and 3) tensions existed about who (northern or southern NGOs) should ultimately govern the monetary inflow of support for Yasuní and its implementation.

Signs of coordination among northern and southern NGOs during 2007 were: a) the two workshops in September and November hosted in Washington, D.C., and Quito, respectively, to discuss the ITT proposal and plans, b) its presentation to the Clinton Global Initiative, and c) the proposal presentation at the Bali Conference on Climate Change in December 2007. David Batker from Earth Economics in Tacoma, Washington, and Carlos Larrea from La Universidad Andina Simón Bolívar in Quito coordinated the November 26–28, 2007, workshop with members of the Ecuadorian government, including minister of foreign relations María Fernanda Espinosa and Lucia Ruiz Mantilla from the Ministry of Energy and Mines, in addition to various NGO participants from the North and the South.[44] These workshops stimulated high levels of coordination globally and locally for this campaign and the commitment of the actors to devise plans that meet global needs.

Building a Consensus and Institutions in Ecuador

For the national government and for transnational network partners, 2007 was organizationally a tumultuous year. While the government announced with fanfare its plan to keep oil underground, it did not provide institutional support for the initiative in the form of funding or a new office to handle the details and project development of such a massive undertaking. Officially, the initiative was within the Ministry of Foreign Affairs, and the minister's advisor, Lucía Gallardo, (formerly of Acción Ecológica) was in charge of developing the detailed proposal to present to the international community. Additionally, minister of energy and mines, Alberto Acosta, established links with the German Technical Cooperation Fund (GIZ, in German *Deutsche Gesellschaft für Internationale Zusammenarbeit*). The spring of 2007 included two visits to Ecuador of German Bundesstadt parliamentarians to discuss the initiative and Germany's possible support of it. During June 2007 at the official ceremony inaugurating the proposal, representatives from Norway, Spain, and Italy also demonstrated initial interest in the proposal.

However, as planning for the complex mechanisms of financing and guarantees began to unfold throughout the summer and fall of 2007, some cracks in the organizational structure were evident. For example, many NGOs commented that they were very involved in the initial setup of the plan and launch in June 2007. Some, like Amazon Watch, were working within the Ministry of Foreign Affairs doing things like writing briefs for the president and helping manage the press at the Clinton Global Initiative in New York City in September 2007. While various INGOs accompanied President Correa to the Clinton Global Initiative, they observed a lack of coordination on the part of the Ecuadorian government to promote the proposal. One activist commented that the Ecuadorian press secretary went out shopping instead of attending the meeting. Members of the organization Finding Species commented that they felt very "involved in" and "informed of" the initiative. They provided photos of Yasuní National Park for the promotional materials. One NGO said that this was the "first time they had worked *with* the government on an initiative."[45]

On the national government side of the campaign, Lucía Gallardo, general director of the environment in the Ministry of Foreign Affairs, was meeting regularly with national and transnational NGOs, but not making progress on a plan. One member of the working group contended that Ms. Gallardo was "very radical" in her approach to the initiative and maintained that her criticism of the Kyoto Protocol created tension between national and international actors. The perception of anti–Kyoto Protocol arguments may have strained relations with the larger international NGOs, such as The Nature Conservancy (TNC) and Conservation International (CI), which were concerned about how this plan to leave oil underground would apply to Kyoto standards. Still, economist and consultant Joseph Henry Vogel maintains that Gallardo was supportive of his concepts to explore Kyoto mechanisms.[46]

Smaller INGOs and national NGOs commented in interviews that they liked the original proposal to seek global donations to keep oil underground, even if it was not within the Kyoto guidelines. These INGOs, such as Amazon Watch, Finding Species, and Pachamama, all had people on the ground in Quito who had been working in the Amazon for many years. According to one INGO activist in this group, "Quito is very small. How things happened in the beginning had everything to do with trust." However, all interviewees commented that the lack of formal government institutionalization of the initiative negatively impacted the progress of the initiative and confidence in it both nationally and internationally.[47]

Deeper Institutionalization and New Mechanisms

The fall of 2007 was filled with studies and development of the proposal via transnational networks with scientists and INGOs, but by December 2007, minister of foreign affairs María Fernanda Espinosa had resigned and María Isabel Salvador had replaced her. This change in leadership was also a change in institutionalization. By January 2008, an office of the technical secretary for the Yasuní-ITT Initiative was created and Juana Ramos, alternative assembly representative for Alberto Acosta in the Constituent Assembly, was appointed to the position. While internally this heightened a sense of government buy-in for the proposal, actors complained that this created friction between Lucía

Gallardo, the director of the environment, who had previously led the initiative, and Juana Ramos. Furthermore, NGO actors contend that the period from Ms. Ramos's appointment in January through her resignation in June 2008 was a time of estrangement between the government and civil society.

The time period of January through June 2008 differed from the first phase of the initial proposal that was based on the ethical and environmental value of Yasuní to the planet with donations from civil society and collaborating countries. During this second phase of mobilization and institutionalization, Juana Ramos and a consultant, Roberto Salazar (contracted by the Ministry of Foreign Affairs before her tenure as technical secretary), began to consider market alternatives to finance the $350 million that President Correa told them they had to raise by June 2008. Actors involved in the network claim that Ms. Ramos met with oil company executives and other transnational corporations regarding possible financing of the campaign. However, Ms. Ramos contends that she interpreted her most important role as saving Yasuní through raising funds by the president's deadline of June 2008. This included creating the financial mechanisms that would support donations to the initiative. To this end, she claims to have met with holdings companies and the European Union Commission representatives, but not with oil company executives for donations to the project.[48]

Secretary Ramos viewed the Yasuní-ITT Initiative not only as protection of the park's biodiversity, but as "a pilot project toward a new scheme of development for the country."[49] Her goals were to develop the financial skeleton of the proposal and work with civil society and with the local communities to develop the proposal. However, Ramos noted that the June deadline forced her to focus on the financial structure more than she had originally anticipated. After working with Carlos Larrea and the technical advisors, she said that they quickly realized that the only efficient manner to reach the $350 million goal was to sell carbon bonds. This shift from donations and international compensation to carbon bond sales was a significant change in the original intent and original proposal made by Alberto Acosta in March 2007 when he was then minister of energy and mines.[50]

Ramos relayed that there was great international interest in a carbon bond initiative, most specifically from Spain, Norway, Germany, and various European parliamentarians with whom she had met. She travelled to Europe in March 2008 to meet with leaders and gather their reactions to the proposal. The concept was to relate the bond value to the value of the petroleum left underground. This, she said, "was an enticing means of valuing the bond as stock prices for oil were easier to quantify than were other forms of carbon capture that were in the international markets."[51] From that point, various financial companies from Europe were interested in talking with the

Ecuadorian government about the proposal, which may explain the concern from various NGO actors that Ramos was meeting with transnational corporations to donate funds.

While the carbon bond concept generated international interest, on the civil society level, it stirred criticism. Ramos commented that organizations such as Oil Watch, an INGO directed then by Esperanza Martínez of Acción Ecológica, criticized the sale of carbon bonds as a means of promoting the Kyoto Protocol and allowing polluters to keep polluting. However, Ramos asserted that carbon bonds for unextracted oil are not accepted measures under the Kyoto Protocol. Furthermore, Ramos stated:

> We had to make all of it work to fulfill what we called the *proceso de transformación energética* (energy transformation process). A part of the resources raised by the Yasuní-ITT fund was planned to be used in this energy transition process, being conscious that, in the interim, we would stop being an oil producing country; so we must modify the economic system. [The year] 2030 cannot come without a stable process of economic substitution for Ecuadorian dependency on oil; we have to make a change. Therefore, we thought everything was going to be done as was said; besides we believed that environmental services could be an important source of income for the country. I totally share the opinion that not all of the environmental services should have an economic objective, although there are environmental services that can benefit everybody, and one of those is carbon capturing.[52]

The Yasuní-ITT trajectory evolved from a plan for compensation to a plan that would provide new economic bases for Ecuador and create a foundation for an Ecuador "post petrolero." The issue, however, was the economic justification for tying Yasuní's survival to market mechanisms.

When Minister of Foreign Affairs Salvador rejected a meeting with Ramos and representatives with a holding company in Spain in May 2008, Ramos resigned from the technical secretary position. For two weeks or so, Lucía Gallardo assumed the role, but the Administrative and Leadership Council (CAD) was created shortly thereafter with the owner of Metropolitan Touring and former mayor of Quito, Roque Sevilla, as its president. Ramos met with Sevilla, who reviewed her work as technical secretary. Ramos said that she was "very happy" to see the CAD's development of the project.[53]

May 2008 was another tumultuous time for the Yasuní-ITT proposal, despite President Correa's continued promotion of the proposal. On May 12, President Correa presented the proposal to representatives of the fifth Latin American and Caribbean–European Union Summit.[54] On May 21, 2008, OPEC secretary general Abdalla Salem El-Badri visited Ecuador and reviewed the initiative with President Correa.[55] This visit was in response to President

Correa's presentation of the Yasuní-ITT Initiative at the OPEC meeting the year before, when he also proposed a tax on petroleum exports from OPEC countries, later to be called the Correa-Daly tax after ecological economist Herman Daly. The conceptualization of President Correa's speech was assisted by former University of Maryland researcher Max Christian and other members of the NGO working group on the initiative.[56] Thus, while the institutional mechanisms of the proposal inside Ecuador were weak, the campaign continued at the global level.

The Administrative and Leadership Council

In June 2008, President Correa, via executive decree, formed the Consejo Administrativo y Directivo (CAD)—Administrative and Leadership Council—with Roque Sevilla as the president, Francisco Carrión and Yolanda Kakabadse as commission members, Galo Armas as the secretariat, and Carlos Larrea as the technical coordinator. With this new institution, the president also extended the deadline to collect the $350 million for the initiative until September 2008. This deadline was later extended to December 2008, and was finally lifted in February 2009. With the February 2009 executive decree, the Ecuadorian government officially made the Yasuní-ITT Initiative part of its permanent environmental and foreign policy without a deadline for funding collection.[57] The imposition of deadlines for funding was highly criticized by civil society. Outside observers, possible donors, and NGO actors viewed these arbitrary dates as a possible ploy to make it appear that Ecuador supported the proposal, leaving open the possibility of later extracting oil from the ITT block. The decision to make the initiative official policy strengthened the proposal and gave it national and international credibility.

Once the CAD was formed, its initial investigation into international feasibility and acceptance of the proposal took place on a visit to Europe during the summer of 2008. From the fall through December 2008, the CAD reviewed suggestions from its international visits, presenting its revised Yasuní-ITT proposal in December 2008. On a visit to Washington, D.C., on December 16, 2008, Roque Sevilla and Yolanda Kakabadse presented the new plan at the World Resources Institute (WRI) with NGO representatives from The Nature Conservancy, Conservation International, Save America's Forests, Amazon Alliance, Amazon Watch, World Wildlife Fund, and Finding Species, among others. The funding for the initiative, at this point, was directed to the over forty protected areas of Ecuador and to other projects as outlined in the National Development Plan of SENPLADES.

However, the carbon bond initiative had changed. Rather than selling bonds at the price of petroleum, the government proposed to sell Certificates of Guarantee Yasuní (CGY) at the price of non-emitted carbon. Thus, the concept of leaving oil underground, while still central to the proposal, had been transformed to the environmental benefit of avoided emissions. This shift in conceptualization left the proposal still market-driven, yet available through different market vendors. In this case, the CGYs would be traded in carbon markets, principally in the European Union Emissions Trading Scheme (EU ETS). Finally, the CAD also included the original funding sources of contributions from collaborating countries and members of civil society.[58]

In the December 2008 meeting, Sevilla and Kakabadse fielded questions from NGO representatives about the feasibility of such funding sources, given the strict regulations of the EU ETS until 2012 and the extreme fluctuation in the pricing of carbon in the voluntary markets. Others asked about the trust fund for the donations and earnings, and how it would be governed. They asked if there would be an international oversight committee and an international plan for monitoring the implementation of such funds. Furthermore, many wanted to know why Ecuador had not presented the new plan at the UNFCCC Global Climate Change talks in Poznan earlier that month. They questioned whether the Ecuadorian government truly backed this proposal.

Sevilla and Kakabadse explained that President Correa supported the proposal and was planning to announce his commitment in 2009. Until that official acceptance came, they were not at liberty to present the proposal to the UNFCCC. They further relayed their interest in NGO reaction to the plan and any suggestions to strengthen it. Clearly, this trip was one of mutual interest and feedback for the Ecuadorian government and potential donors/transnational network members. This contact with transnational network members was also one of the first opportunities that NGO actors had to hear the new proposal since Juana Ramos had resigned in June 2008.

The Ping-Pong Policy Approach

With this new plan and a strengthened institutional anchor to the initiative, the Yasuní-ITT campaign seemed as though it would gain momentum in 2009. However, by January 2009, minister of mining and petroleum, Derlis Palacios, announced future bidding for the ITT block, stating that "If we find an immediate solution [for keeping oil underground], we will consider it. I think that we have already lost good time. We will make every necessary attempt to protect the environment, but the country needs money."[59] The next day, newly appointed minister of foreign affairs, Fander Falconí, apologized for the "miscommunication" and stated that this was not the government plan. President Correa, following that announcement, endorsed leaving oil underground with an executive decree that made the Yasuní-ITT proposal official foreign policy for the country without a deadline.[60]

However, the ping pong of Plan A and Plan B had drained much of the energy from the transnational networks' actors. Many were skeptical of government plans and had disconnected from the initiative during the fall of 2008. Complicating the ITT issue was block 31, which is next to the ITT block within Yasuní National Park and the Waorani Ethnic Reserve. Initially, it looked as though Petrobras would begin oil extraction in that block in 2008. However, in September 2008, Petrobras returned the block to the Ecuadorian government. During this time frame, however, the international community and transnational network actors lost their confidence in the ITT proposal because the president seemed disposed to drill for oil within the park just next to the ITT block.[61]

Global-Local Nexus toward a Revised Yasuní-ITT Proposal

The CAD contracted a series of studies during the spring of 2009 regarding the legal, financial, and environmental elements of the Yasuní-ITT proposal that it presented in December 2008. Funding from the German International Cooperation Enterprise financed the consultations that were presented at a government workshop in Puembo, Ecuador, in March 2008 to review the findings. While nearly two years after the initial announcement of the initiative one would have expected a finalization of the proposal with a clear strategy to disseminate it worldwide, the Puembo meeting demonstrated the CAD's indecision on its financial mechanisms.

International consultants from Climate Focus, Katoomba, and Silvestrum presented their findings, which all agreed that the carbon trading markets would be difficult avenues of finance for the project because the EU ETS had already established guidelines through 2012, which did not include CGYs. Some discussed US market potential with possible future US legislation on climate change. Following this discussion, participants from the technical advisory committee discussed other funding options, such as CGYs to guarantee debt forgiveness and international loans (an idea which was quickly rejected). At the conclusion of the meeting, Roque Sevilla thanked everyone and asked if they could meet one more time to review other funding options. Still, Sevilla remained positive and asked everyone to "think outside the box" about this proposal. He understood the difficulties and challenges of it, but preferred to focus on its pioneering possibilities.[62]

Over the course of the next few weeks, the proposal was revised a final time to include CGYs as a guarantee for debt forgiveness and to reduce emphasis on carbon markets. The key element of the previous proposal of avoided or non-emitted emissions remained, yet now in payment for debt forgiveness or through voluntary carbon markets, rather than the EU ETS. A renewed emphasis on collaborating country and civil society donations was also included. One transnational actor involved in the discussions commented that CAD president Roque Sevilla was determined to make the proposal work. Rather than dwelling on misgivings, he emphasized the positive and included aspects that actors from civil society had favored.[63] The CAD worked tirelessly on this new version, including Sunday meetings at personal residences and evening conferences.

Part of the impetus for reform of the proposal was from international consultants. However, a significant catalyst for change came from civil society. Many transnational actors were critical of the carbon market emphasis. They preferred aspects of preserving Yasuní for environmental-ethical reasons, not just for its economic value. Former minister of energy and mines, Alberto Acosta, Esperanza Martínez of Acción Ecológica, Joseph Henry Vogel from La Facultad Latinoamericana de Ciencias Sociales (FLACSO), and Uruguayan academic Eduardo Gudynas released a critique of the proposal in the spring of 2009, which was later published in English in the United States as well. They emphasized alternative forms of funding and Ecuador's responsibility to protect Yasuní without market reinforcements. Yet, if post-Kyoto discussions were to include limits on fuel consumption or means of accounting for reduced emissions of oil left underground, the authors offered market and non-market solutions and mechanisms for global opportunities for the Yasuní-ITT Initiative and beyond.[64] Their close relationship with La Universidad Andina economist Carlos Larrea, the CAD technical coordinator, and other currents from civil society supporting them, influenced the final CAD version of the Yasuní-ITT proposal.

Following the release in May 2009 of the revised proposal, CAD members travelled internationally to gain support. Yolanda Kakabadse visited Joe Aldy, US special assistant on energy and climate change in the White House in May 2009. Later that month, Alberto Acosta presented the plan to the German Committee on Economic and Development Cooperation. In June 2009, the CAD met with German officials, ending in unanimous support for the proposal by the Bundestag. Other meetings took place in Great Britain and Italy as well. By September 2009, the German government had pledged $50 million over thirteen years to the initiative and Spanish officials were considering a plan to pledge $20 million over the same time period.[65] Ecuadorian ambassador to the United Nations, María Fernanda Espinosa, (the former minister of foreign affairs who worked on initial stages of the proposal) was working on the financial structure of the trust fund with the UNDP.

The long road to the final proposal of the Yasuní-ITT Initiative is a story of local and global interactions with dedicated civil society members. Ironically, the final version of the proposal looks very similar to its original form, yet with critical additions of CGYs and market options for funding. The process of getting to the final version included bumps along the way of lack of institutional commitment and varying degrees of communication with civil society. Still, few meetings have been held with members of the Waorani peoples and local leaders and park officials. However, the creation of the CAD and its weaving of local and international norms and mechanisms, in addition to high levels of dialog among actors, have produced an innovative policy option for Ecuadorian people and the international community.

Notes

1. Interministerial Decree No. 322, published in the Official Register No. 69 (November 20, 1979).

2. Guillaume Fontaine and Iván Narváez, *Yasuní en el siglo XXI: El Estado ecuatoriano y la conservación de la Amazonía* (Quito, Ecuador: FLACSO, 2007), 22; Matt Finer et al., "Ecuador's Yasuní Biosphere Reserve: A Brief Modern History and Conservation Challenges," *IOP Publishing Environmental Research*, July–September 2009, 7.

3. Matt Finer, C. N. Jenkins, S. L. Pimm, B. Keane, and C. Ross,"Oil and Gas Projects in the Western Amazon: Threats to Wilderness, Biodiversity, and Indigenous Peoples," *PLoS ONE* 3, no. 8 (2008), e2932. doi:10.1371/journal.pone.0002932.

4. This is a group of international scientists whose work was spearheaded by Save America's Forests, an international environmental NGO.

5. Finer et al., "Ecuador's Yasuní Biosphere Reserve," 7–8; Bass et al., "Global Conservation Significance of Ecuador's Yasuní National Park," *PLoS ONE* 5, no. 1 (2010): e8767.

6. Matt Finer and Pamela Martin, "Ecuador's Amazon-sized Challenge to the World: Part I," *Globalist* 2010, http://www.theglobalist.com/storyid.aspx?StoryId=8527 (accessed on December 12, 2010).

7. Finer et al., "Ecuador's Yasuní Biosphere Reserve"; Beckerman et al., "Life Histories, Blood Revenge, and Reproductive Success among the Waorani of Ecuador," *Proceedings of the National Academy of Sciences of the United States* 107, no. 45 (2010): 19195–19200.

8. Laura Rival, *Trekking through History* (Cambridge: Cambridge University Press, 2002).

9. "Los Pueblos Ocultos Siguen Acosados," *El Comercio*, August 22, 2009.

10. Esperanza Martínez, "Yasuní: Mas de 100 Buenas Razones para NO Sacar el Petróleo," *Amazonía por la Vida*, November 2008, 69–70.

11. Executive Decree 552 in the Official Register.

12. Miguel Angel Cabodevilla, "Pueblos ocultos en Ecuador," *Llacta!* November 2006; Finer et al., "Ecuador's Yasuní Biosphere Reserve"; Andrés Jaramillo, "Los pueblos ocultos siguen acosados," *El Comercio*, August 23, 2009.

13. Cabodevilla, "Pueblos ocultos en Ecuador"; Finer et al., "Ecuador's Yasuní Biosphere Reserve"; Martínez, "Yasuní."

14. Guillaume Fontaine, *El Precio del Petróleo* (Quito, Ecuador: Abya Yala, 2007), 76.

15. Fontaine and Narváez, *Yasuní en el siglo XXI*, 16.

16. Fontaine, *El Precio del Petróleo*, 86.

17. Fontaine, *El Precio del Petróleo*, 90.

18. Ricardo Crespo, "Yasuní en el siglo XXI: El Estado ecuatoriano y la conservación en la Amazonía," in *Yasuní en el siglo XXI: El Estado ecuatoriano y la conservación en la Amazonía*, ed. Guillaume Fontaine and Iván Narváez (Quito, Ecuador: Abya Yala, 2007), 45.

19. Fontaine, *El Precio del Petróleo.*

20. Interviews with author, Quito, Ecuador, spring 2009.

21. Fontaine, *El Precio del Petróleo*, 225.

22. Iván Narváez, "La política ambiental del Estado: Hacia el colapso del modelo de conservación?" in *Yasuní en el siglo XXI: El Estado ecuatoriano y la conservación en la Amazonía*, ed. Guillaume Fontaine and Iván Narváez (Quito, Ecuador: Abya Yala, 2007), 55.

23. Esperanza Martínez, "De Kyoto a Quito," *Llacta!*, May 9, 2007.

24. "Crude Oil and Total Petroleum Imports Top 15 Countries," *Energy Information Administration*, September 29, 2009, http://www.eia.doe.gov/pub/oil_gas/petroleum/data_publications/company_level_imports/current/import.html.

25. This information is from an independent report from the Beicip Franlab (2004) as contracted by Petroproducción (Carlos Larrea et al., "Yasuní-ITT Initiative a Big Idea from a Small Country," 2009, 12); Martínez, "Yasuní."

26. Larrea et al., "Yasuní-ITT Initiative," 12. http://www.yasuni-itt.gov.ec/download/Yasuni_ITT_Initiative1009.pdf.

27. Mauricio Dávila, interview with author, Quito, Ecuador, March 24, 2009. Translation by author.

28. Ibid.

29. Ibid.

30. B. Metz et al., *Climate Change 2007: Mitigation. Contribution of Working Group III to the Fourth Assessment Report of the Intergovernmental Panel on Climate Change*, IPCC (New York: Cambridge University Press, 2007).

31. William Langewiesche, "Jungle Law," *Vanity Fair*, May 4, 2007, http://www.vanityfair.com/politics/features/2007/05/texaco200705.

32. J. Kimerling, *Amazon Crude* (New York: Natural Resources Defense Council, 1991).

33. Martínez, "De Kyoto a Quito."

34. Alberto Acosta, "El petróleo en el Ecuador: Una evaluación critica del pasado cuarto del siglo," *El Ecuador Post Petrolero* (Quito: Acción Ecológica, Idlis, and Oilwatch, 2000).

35. Esperanza Martínez, "Dejar el Crudo en Tierra en el Yasuní—Un Reto a la Coherencia," *Revista Tendencia* 9 (April 2009): 1–13.

36. Rafael Correa, "Yasuní-ITT," last modified May 30, 2009, http://www.youtube.com/user/YasuniITT#p/a/f/0/_dg48IM9gwM (accessed December 20, 2009).

37. "Avatar in the Amazon," *The World*, PRI, January 29, 2010, http://www.theworld.org/2010/01/29/avatar-in-the-amazon/.

38. Martínez, "Dejar el Crudo en Tierra."

39. Rafael Correa, "Speech of the President of Ecuador; High Level Dialogue on Climate Change of the 62 Period of Sessions of the General Assembly of the United Nations," September 24, 2007, http://www.ecuador.org/bulletin_board/relative_docs/ letter_climatechange.pdf.

40. Max Christian, telephone interview, June 21, 2007.

41. As economist Joseph Henry Vogel keenly observes, the "United Nations has so many international conventions, and post-Kyoto is about climate change, and not specifically about human rights and biodiversity." Personal communication with author.

42. See also Charli Carpenter, "Studying Issue (Non)-Adoption in Transnational Advocacy Networks," *International Organization* 61, no. 3 (2007): 643–667.

43. Mitch Anderson, telephone interview, August 10, 2007.

44. Ministerio de Relaciones Exteriores, Comercio e Integración, "Encuentro Taller-Iniciativa Yasuní-ITT," Vicepresidencia de la República, Ministerio de Relaciones Exteriores, Comercio e Integración, Universidad Andina Simón Bolívar, Earth Economics, World Resources Institute, November 21–23, 2007, http://www .eartheconomics.org/FileLibrary/file/Reports/Summary_of_Yasun%C3%AD_ITT _Conference.pdf.

45. Interviews in Quito, spring 2009.

46. Joseph Henry Vogel, e-mail message to author, 2010.

47. Interviews in Quito, spring 2009.

48. Juana Ramos, interview, Quito, Ecuador, March 6, 2009.

49. Ibid.

50. Alberto Acosta became the president of the Constituent Assembly to rewrite the constitution in 2008.

51. Ramos, interview, Quito, Ecuador, March 6, 2009.

52. Ibid. Translation by author.

53. Ibid.

54. "Correa Expondrá en la Cumbre ALC-UE su plan para dejar crudo en tierra," *El Comercio*, May 12, 2008.

55. "Secretario General de la OPEP Visita Ecuador Interesado en le Proyecto ITT," *El Comercio*, May 20, 2008.

56. Christian, telephone interview, June 21, 2007.

57. Executive Decree No. 1572.

58. Roque Sevilla, "The Yasuní-ITT: An Innovative Model to Save the Planet," presentation, November 2008.

59. "Campo ITT irá a licitación internacional," *Diario Hoy*, January 9, 2009.

60. "El Regimen Congela la Explotacion en el Yasuní," *El Comercio*, February 14, 2009.

61. Verónica Quitigüiña, interview, Quito, Ecuador, March 4, 2009.

62. Participant observation.

63. Roque Sevilla, telephone interview, Quito, Ecuador, February 5, 2009.

64. Alberto Acosta et al., "A Political, Economic, and Ecological Initiative in the Ecuadorian Amazon," Americas Program Policy Report, August 13, 2009.

65. "Correa aboga por carretera Manta-Manaos," *El Universo*, September 30, 2009.

4

Pay to Preserve

The Yasuní-ITT Trust Fund

WHILE THE YASUNÍ-ITT CAMPAIGN seemed headed toward success in the UN Climate Change talks of Copenhagen in December 2009, at the last minute, President Correa refused to sign the trust fund agreement with the United Nations Development Programme (UNDP) to guarantee its funding. On December 14, 2009, just two days before the scheduled signing by Ecuadorian government officials and UNDP representatives, President Rafael Correa sent a message via e-mail to his team in Copenhagen not to sign the agreement that had been in high-level negotiations for months. Not surprisingly, the team was nonplussed.

During his weekly radio address on January 9, President Correa criticized the team for accepting conditions in the UNDP trust fund that were "shameful" and "threatened the sovereignty" of their country. On January 27, President Correa declared, "We are the ones who have to put the conditions" in the trust fund. He claimed that the negotiating committee's error was in the terms of reference. Correa said, "We are not asking for charity, but for just compensation for environmental services."[1] The word "donor" in the UNDP trust fund stuck in his craw.

The global governance mechanisms of what could be the largest global environmental trust fund have been controversial for Ecuador. Yet the debate and disagreement about the UNDP trust fund also highlights the significance of negotiation and bargaining in the global governance process. In response to President Correa's remarks in January 2009, CAD president Roque Sevilla, commission member Yolanda Kakabadse, and minister of foreign affairs

Fander Falconí resigned. Falconí said after his resignation, "Evidently, there are oil interests that want to drill."[2]

Nevertheless, President Correa has publicly stated that he supports the proposal to keep oil underground. By February 2010, new leadership assumed the helm of the CAD with vice president Lenin Moreno and Ivonne Baki as CAD president. Former minister of foreign affairs and now minister of national and cultural heritage, María Fernanda Espinosa, is also a member of the new CAD. Moreno and Baki, unlike their predecessors who focused on European alliances, began their tenure by travelling to the Middle East for support and funding of the Yasuní-ITT Initiative. By August 2010, in addition to Germany, Spain, France, and Belgium, the United Arab Emirates, Iran, and OPEC have officially announced their support of the initiative. Furthermore, Minister Espinosa and CAD President Baki announced a new global tour of the Yasuní-ITT Trust Fund to entice contributors scheduled for the fall of 2010 and into 2011.

While the delay of the Yasuní-ITT UNDP Trust Fund (Yasuní Fund abbreviated) formalization until August 3, 2010, could have been a signal that President Correa was opting to drill for oil in the ITT block, it was also a lesson in global governance. As witnessed throughout the 2009 Copenhagen talks, the Bolivian Climate Change and Mother Earth conference in Cochabamba in 2010, and May 2010 agreements for energy between Iran and Brazil, the South is pushing back. Riding this tide, President Correa is asserting Ecuador's sovereign voice in the governance of funding for the Yasuní-ITT Initiative. Such a press for power from the South may be the trend in global governance on climate change initiatives, given the severe impact of industrialized nations on the climate—specifically carbon emissions—and the grave effects on countries in the South like Ecuador.

How Much Money Will This Cost and Where Does It All Come From?

Instead of earning money from oil extraction, Ecuador will earn its money from avoided carbon emissions and the projects that will result from related contributions. Of special note to this proposal is the difference in direction of the funds. According to Carlos Larrea, technical advisor to the CAD, while oil money goes into the coffers of the national government, these funds will go directly to national development projects, which will specifically be determined in advance of fund disbursement.[3] The 2008 constitution considers control of natural resources and the provisions of environmental services to be functions of national sovereignty.[4] Yet this new element to project financing adds a global dimension, as the fund is administered with the United Nations, which has the effect of decentralizing the flow of income to the country.

In his book *The Economics of the Yasuní Initiative*, Joseph Henry Vogel, however, argues that fungibility is a significant issue to overcome for the funds contributed to the Yasuní Trust Fund. Rather than contributing to public good projects already funded by the government, Vogel argues that projects of a unique nature that would not have already been funded by the state should be funded. This, he argues, ensures that Yasuní Trust Fund contributions do not replace government funding of public projects in the state's interest, but rather fund innovative and sustainable initiatives that move toward an increase in Ecuador's ranking in the Human Development Index (HDI).[5] This United Nations quality of life index ranks Ecuador in seventy-seventh place. Vogel would tie funding of the initiative to a rise in Ecuador's ranking equivalent to that of Costa Rica, which is in the sixty-second place among 169 countries.[6] Such a mechanism is not included in the August 2010 Yasuní-ITT Trust Fund terms of reference or memorandum of agreement, but Vogel's concept for tying contributions to real outcomes for a sustainable future should be seriously considered by members of the Trust Fund Steering Committee.

The Ecuadorian government expects to receive this funding for the Yasuní Trust Fund over a ten-year time period, which is the amount of time it estimates it would extract approximately 107,000 barrels of oil per day. This does not, however, include the five years or so that experts estimate it would take to prepare the field for extraction and transportation.[7] Thus, keeping the oil underground in this Amazonian block would provide an immediate source of sustainable funding for the country, as well as an opportunity to transition the economy from one that is oil dependent to one that produces renewable energy.

The Contributions

The contributions to this fund are expected to begin in late 2010–2011 and will be derived from two sources primarily: 1) voluntary contributions from individuals, public and private organizations, and governments, and 2) voluntary carbon markets and possibly the European Union Emissions Trading Scheme (EU ETS) through the sale of Certificados de Garantía Yasuní (CGYs) to public and private entities. The funding for this project is linked to national and international debates about the price of nature and biodiversity, and the value of ecosystems, specifically the Amazon, to future generations. This proposal also revitalizes the global conversation on "ecological debt" in an innovative manner. Former CAD president Roque Sevilla noted "If a US citizen emits each year 19.73 tons of CO_2 against the 1.68 tons that an Ecuadorian emits, and we consider that one ton of CO_2 is worth \$10 and the average world emission rates is 4.18 tons, then the United States would have a debt of \$45.7 million annually, while Ecuador would have a credit of \$325 million per year."[8]

Yet the Yasuní-ITT proposal goes beyond debt to co-responsibility. Acosta et al. argue for a "common, but differentiated responsibility" between industrialized and developing countries. Transcending the usual argument that the North should pay for destroying the South, they contend there is a co-responsibility in which the North, having become wealthy through a dirty industrialization, should contribute to the protection of nature with countries from the South. In return, the Ecuadorian state has the responsibility to protect its treasured areas with policies that reflect sustainable development and "the good life," regardless of whether there is financing.[9]

Another option for financing, related to government contributions, would be debt swaps with the guarantee of Certificados de Garantía Yasuní-ITT (CGYs). According to Sevilla, "Each year we plan to sell 5 percent of this amount [meaning total amount of their yearly contributions] to each country, according to their gross domestic product. What will be sold are Certificados de Garantía Yasuní-ITT that also will apply to debt cancellation. Of the nearly 500 million dollars of Ecuador's debt, the Paris Club has a certain amount of bonds, and what we would do is exchange them for Certificados de Garantía Yasuní-ITT."[10] This aspect of the financing plan goes beyond Ecuador's already-established history with debt-for-nature swaps to a new frontier in nature guarantees of *non*-extracted fossil fuels and *non*-emitted carbon dioxide. Some countries, such as Spain, have communicated their interest in contributing to the Yasuní Fund via this mode of payment and guarantee.[11]

Another possible source of contribution to the Yasuní-ITT campaign would entail funds derived from emission permit auctions or carbon taxes. In the case of emission permits, industries receive a certain quota of emission allowances free of charge, but then have to purchase any further emission permits via auctioning. The funds derived from these auctions can be donated to the Yasuní-ITT campaign, for instance. Germany, the main supporter of this proposal, is calling for such auctions, as well as the European Union for post-2012 policies. Additionally, the US government is considering a cap-and-trade system that will auction about 15 percent of emissions permits. The revenue from these auctions could also support this initiative.

Carbon taxes are paid by polluters for their environmental damage and would be another source of revenue. In the policy mix of carbon emissions abatement, countries such as Denmark, Finland, Norway, and Sweden also employ such taxation. Norway, in particular, has been a vocal supporter of the Yasuní-ITT proposal, having hosted various visits from Ecuadorian officials. These sources of income would be derived from polluting industries in the industrialized world yet would be invested in the protection of biodiversity in the ITT block of the Amazon and throughout the country.

The Yasuní-ITT Fund Mechanisms

Aside from general contributions from partner countries and international organizations, there are three other possible sources of revenue generation built into this plan outside of carbon markets. The first of these would be direct investment in renewable energy, which will be financed by the Capital Fund Window of the Ecuador-UNDP Yasuní-ITT Trust Fund. These renewable energy projects, such as hydroelectric, geothermal, wind, and solar energies, are projected to earn profits, which would be placed into a second fund—the Revenue Fund. The Revenue Fund will be used to fund development projects in the areas of deforestation and conservation of ecosystems; reforestation and afforestation; renewable energy and national energy efficiency; social development in the initiative's zones of influence; and support for research, science, technology, and innovation. These areas of development have been specified within the National Development Plan.[12]

As part of his analysis of the Yasuní Initiative and funding mechanisms, economist Joseph Henry Vogel recommends that specific projects be determined in advance of these broad categories. He suggests a Pan-American Ciclovía (bike path) with eco-lodges along the path; collapse tourism in which tourists view sites of ecological degradation and ecological preservation in Ecuador as a means of changing political values; and a carbon tax paid at the airport.[13] As the Yasuní Trust Fund is in its infancy, no specific projects have been detailed. However, Vogel's suggestions and others as determined by local communities would guarantee innovative and sustainable projects well beyond the life of the trust fund. Such projects would likely be a part of the Revenue Fund as outlined in the Yasuní Fund Funding flow chart (figure 4.1).

While the August 2010 Yasuní Trust Fund does not mention options of coordination with other international climate change agreements, previous fund discussions included them. The deforestation project aim would be to eliminate such destruction within a thirty-year time period and end one of the region's highest deforestation rates of 198,000 hectares per year.[14] The energy projects would fall under the current Kyoto Protocol CDM, while the forestation projects could become part of the proposed REDD post-Kyoto agreements. It was not clear as of August 2010 how the new UNDP Yasuní Fund agreement would integrate with other initiatives. The Ecuadorian government, however, estimates that additional projects would mitigate approximately 820 million metric tons of carbon for our planet.[15]

Voluntary contributions would also be accepted from civil society organizations, such as foundations, NGOs, educational or research institutions, and others. Additionally, socially and environmentally responsible private companies would be encouraged to contribute to this trust fund. The role of corporations would be controversial, however, because some leaders of the initiative, such as Alberto Acosta, Esperanza Martínez, and former foreign minister and economist Fander Falconí, have openly criticized transnational corporations and their role in the social and environmental destruction of the Amazon.[16]

Finally, Ecuadorian leaders enthusiastically endorsed one final mode of voluntary contribution: those from citizens worldwide. This method of monetary contribution via the click of a button provides the campaign global ownership, argue the CAD (former and current CAD officials) and other leaders. They also contend that it will form a civil society base that will protect Yasuní and pressure Ecuador to expand its coverage to neighboring Block 31, and eventually the entire park.[17]

While a previous version of this proposal emphasized carbon markets, including voluntary carbon markets and the EU ETS, the final version of the proposal integrates this form of funding without relying on it completely. First, there were technical issues with integration into the EU ETS as non-emitted carbon does not qualify under the Kyoto Protocol as Certified Emissions Reductions (CERs) under the CDM. The EU ETS trades certified carbon credits as part of the European Union allowance for carbon emissions limitations of member nations. These rules have been put in place until 2012, when the Kyoto Protocol regulations expire.

For the carbon credits to work, Ecuador would have to become a pilot case for the EU ETS, which is highly unlikely given the political hurdles of changing EU policy so quickly, according to consultants for the CAD. Second, only industrialized Annex 1 countries participate in such carbon credits. This limits the marketplace to participating members, of which the EU ETS is the only non-voluntary emissions trading system—outside of regional systems such as that of California. The Ecuadorian government did consider the voluntary marketplace as an option, but recognized its limitations as prices tend to be lower and fluctuate more. However, such voluntary status may change if the United States and other countries adopt cap-and-trade systems that accept CGYs within the trading mechanism.

While the Yasuní Fund has included a market-based approach as part of the funding strategy, others in civil society, globally and nationally, argue that the Amazon has been subjected to international oil markets for years and its

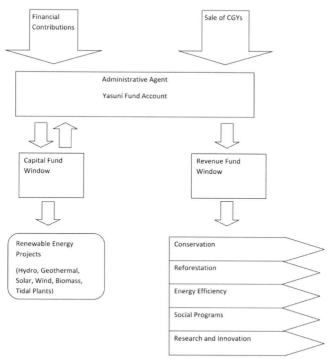

FIGURE 4.1
Yasuní Fund Funding Flow

Source: National government of Ecuador and United Nations Development Programme, Ecuador Yasuní-ITT Trust Fund: Terms of Reference. Available at http://mdtf.undp.org/document/search?fund=3EY00&document_areas=fund,project&go=true, p. 7.

natural resources have dwindled. Rather than subject it to further pricing on its known commodities, the Ecuadorian state should make it a national policy to stop all exploration and drilling in the entire park and uncontacted zone (ZI—*zona intangible* in Spanish) as an ethical policy testament to its commitment to sustainable development and "the good life." Part of this argument is that the market can only account for known ecosystem services, such as carbon dioxide emissions and decreased deforestation, whereas the benefits from other forms of biodiversity as yet to be discovered, of cultural and ethnic diversity and preservation, and to future generations are not intrinsically commensurable and are therefore, beyond the market.[18] As Alberto Acosta et al. poignantly explain:

> [W]e believe that protecting life cannot be done through market forces. Putting a monetary value on nature, in other words life, is not the most adequate

TABLE 4.1
Sources of Funding for the Yasuní-ITT Initiative:

Non-market-based	Market-based
Debt-for-conservation swaps	Emissions permits
Government contributions	Carbon taxes
Civil society organization contributions	EU ETS
Socially and environmentally responsible	
private companies	Voluntary carbon markets
Citizens	
Contributions to specific projects	

measurement, it seems to us. Thus, the ITT proposal undermines the essence of the carbon market, the essence of the Kyoto Protocol. For this reason, this project outlines a post-Kyoto logic.

With this non-extraction of oil, we plan to reinvent the international agenda on climate change: speaking of petroleum and its excessive consumption as a principal agent of these phenomena, impelling practical actions in which we put in play the common, but differentiated responsibilities, positioning in the international/global agenda the importance of biodiversity conservation and respect for the rights of indigenous peoples.[19]

From Kyoto to Quito: Who Governs and How?

"But what we are thinking goes beyond Kyoto and to Quito. Our idea is a break from the past; ITT opens up a different panorama." —Alberto Acosta[20]

On January 2, 2008, President Rafael Correa approved Executive Decree 847 for the establishment of a trust fund for the Yasuní-ITT Initiative, called the Fund for Energy Transition Yasuní-ITT (FMTE), which is governed by the trust fund board under the directorship of the National Finance Corporation (CNF). The decree recognizes Ecuador as a megadiverse country and the responsibility that corresponds to protecting such an environment.[21]

As of August 2010, the fund has only ever received $3,300 in total in both its international and national bank accounts.[22] Support for this initiative was given in the form of 300,000 Euros from the German government for technical studies and $200,000 from the UNDP for project studies and information diffusion.[23] In addition, President Correa decreed a $1,000 donation in support of the initiative on January 2, 2008. The operating budget for the initiative, which includes studies and honoraria for board members in 2008, was $1 million.[24] CAD (current and former) members have asked for increased funding.[25] The theoretical and financial foundations for the Yasuní-ITT Initiative and its subsequent trust fund are based on concepts of shared responsibility with the international community and in accordance with international agreements, in addition to the direct funding of the project from Germany and the UNDP (through a special fund for climate change donated by Spain). In a decree to lift the time frame to collect funding in February 2009, President Correa also highlighted the Yasuní-ITT project as "emblematic" of Ecuador's environmental policy, which emphasizes that its citizens have the right to "live in a safe and ecologically sound environment that guarantees sustainability and the good life."[26]

Domestic Institutional Organization and Participation

Separate from financial governance of the initiative, President Correa has created significant governmental institutions with special regard to this project. In January 2008, an Office of the Technical Secretary for the Yasuní-ITT Initiative was inaugurated within the Ministry of Foreign Affairs with a special presidential representative to the Yasuní-ITT Initiative. Juana Ramos served as technical secretary until June 2008 and former minister of foreign affairs/current Ecuadorian ambassador to the UN, Francisco Carrión, became the president's special representative. To strengthen the coordination among governmental ministries, President Correa also created the Inter-ministerial Council on the Yasuní-ITT Initiative, which is composed of the ministers and/or secretaries of foreign affairs, finances, political economy, environment, mines and petroleum (now called the Ministry of Non-renewable Resources), natural and cultural heritage, tourism, electricity and renewable energy, and national planning and development.[27]

The fact that President Correa originally located the technical secretary and the entire initiative within the Ministry of Foreign Affairs is important because it emphasizes both the global nature of this project and the high level and prestige placed upon it within the administration. While Ecuador does have an Environmental Ministry, it is relatively new (1996) and less powerful than the Ministry of Foreign Affairs. Moreover, Ambassador Carrión is a well-respected and longtime diplomat for the country, which speaks to the serious nature of this proposal.

Under the newly adopted governance structure with the UNDP to be discussed below, President Correa has moved the Yasuní-ITT leadership team from the Ministry of Foreign Affairs to the Ministry of Natural and Cultural Heritage. While previously called the CAD, the new domestic arm of governance of the initiative is called the Government Coordinating Entity. This entity will work in conjunction with the Yasuní Fund Steering Committee and with the Yasuní Fund Technical Secretariat. These domestic institutional changes signal the importance of the initiative in the Correa administration and the domestic-international linkages within the new Yasuní Fund governance structure.

The Government Coordinating Entity is composed of:

a) the president (originally Roque Sevilla, former mayor of Quito and director of environmental NGO Fundación Natura; currently Ivonne Baki, president of the Andean Parliament);
b) the minister of foreign affairs (first María Isabel Salvador, second Fander Falconí—an ecological economist—and as of December 2010 Ricardo Patiño, also an economist);
c) the presidential representative (former foreign affairs minister, Francisco Carrión);
d) a national and international civil society representative (former minister of the environment, Yolanda Kakabadse, until January 2010; as of December 2010 María Fernanda Espinosa, minister of cultural heritage); and
e) in February 2010, vice president Lenin Moreno also assumed leadership of the initiative.

The elevation of the Yasuní-ITT Initiative within the governmental structure has not been without controversy. Many actors, including NGOs and supporting countries, criticized Ecuador's slow pace on the initiative and lack of clear policies for financing and governance. From the January 2008 decree through June 2008, the government had also toggled between its Plan A: "Save Yasuní-ITT," and its Plan B: "Drill in ITT if funds are not collected." This policy tug discredited the government and lowered confidence in the initiative for those who supported it.[28] For those who question why anyone should contribute to the Yasuní-ITT Trust Fund, the answer is simple: if we do not, the pressures to develop the ITT oil field will become insurmountable. As Joseph Henry Vogel points out, saving Yasuní is not avoiding the emissions of a China or India, but it is an excellent "second-best option," as many policies in place today have been.[29]

In a country whose economy is driven by petro-dollars with a state-run oil company, Petroecuador, the battle between those who want to drill for oil and those who do not is an obvious one, even within the president's cabinet. While such debates between Plans A and B have now quieted since the lifting of the deadline for funds on February 5, 2009, the historical place of Petroecuador within the governmental hierarchy is significant. Scholars such as Ricardo Crespo, Iván Narváez, and Guillaume Fontaine have keenly observed the high level of political power that Petroecuador and its executive president wield. Alberto Acosta, who in 2007 was minister of energy and mines, noted that even as president of the board of Petroecuador he was challenged by the executive director, Carlos Pareja Yannuzzelli, who preferred to sign agreements to extract oil from the ITT block.

According to Acosta, the Ministry reviewed means of extracting petroleum from this block with engineers, but recognized the technical difficulty of such a feat due to its heavy nature (14.7 API), which would require processing in Lago Agrio or Shushufindi to the North and the need for an electricity plant. From the standpoint of engineering, the project is quite a challenge, but in further cost analysis, it turns out to be quite expensive. Regardless, Pareja Yannuzzelli accelerated his pace for contracts in the ITT block as Acosta gained support from President Correa to leave oil underground in return for international compensation.

In a meeting with the president and the cabinet ministers in 2007 in Guayaquil, Acosta gave out T-shirts to the ministers with the slogan, "Yasuní is our oxygen: No to Petroleum from ITT, Yes to Life." When President Correa saw the slogan on the T-shirts, he became very upset and told his ministers that if they wanted to wear such shirts, they should resign. Acosta kept his shirt on. The president retorted that this slogan was difficult to defend because if someday they did extract oil from this area, it would imply that it was a policy against human life. Acosta discussed the issue with the president and, eventually, resigned from his cabinet position to direct the Constitutional Assembly in Montecristi. However, this story relays the inter-institutional struggle between those maintaining traditional petro-power and those representing a post-petroleum Ecuador.[30]

Global Governance: The Yasuní Fund

In light of President Correa's criticisms of the original UNDP trust fund negotiations in January 2010, the agreed upon global governance structures have been altered to emphasize Ecuadorian sovereignty over the initiative. These changes, as noted in table 4.2, include an additional Ecuadorian government representative and two representatives from contributing countries.

TABLE 4.2
Changes to the Yasuní Fund Steering Committee

Original Trust Fund Configuration *(Pre-January 2010)*	*Yasuní Fund UNDP Terms* *(August 3, 2010)*
2 government representatives	3 government representatives
1 civil society representative	1 civil society representative
1 contributor representative	2 contributor representatives
1 technical secretary with no vote	1 technical secretary with no vote

The civil society representative remains in place, but the voting process has changed. While majority voting on issues within the Yasuní Fund UNDP Steering Committee was originally accepted, the August 3, 2010, memorandum of agreement between Ecuador and the UNDP outlines consensus voting, if there is not a majority vote. President Correa has stated that Ecuador's government reserves the right to make all final trust fund decisions.

The Yasuní Fund Steering Committee will be responsible for the oversight and direction of the fund. It will review and make allocation decisions from both the Capital and Revenue Funds, as recommended by the Government Coordinating Entity and the Technical Secretariat. It will authorize the release of funds to recipient and implementing organizations and it will review and prepare an annual strategic plan for the fund. In addition to third-party auditing oversight of the fund, as commissioned by the Steering Committee, it will also be responsible for monitoring and evaluation of the Yasuní Fund through an external "lessons learned" report. The Steering Committee will set the minimum threshold for reimbursement in the event that the government should drill for oil in the ITT block, as well as designate the minimum amount of contributions that will warrant the issuance of CGYs.

All proposals for funding from recipient organizations out of the Revenue Fund or from implementing entities from the Capital Fund (for renewable energy projects only) will first be vetted by the Government Coordinating Entity in consultation with the Technical Secretariat (which is an independent body with no vote) before going on to the approval stage by the Steering Committee. This structure favors Ecuadorian government control over the funding, while also ensuring global governance mechanisms and oversight. An important caveat to this structure is that only national entities may receive funding from the Yasuní Fund for projects. This may have to be amended as technical consulting and other services may be required of international entities, such as in the case of renewable energy projects.[31]

Guarantees, Monitoring, and Evaluation

According to Alberto Acosta, former president of the Constitutional Assembly of 2008, the constitution prohibits the extraction of natural resources in protected areas. However, this is controversial, as there are oil blocks located within Yasuní National Park and the government in 2007 and 2008 had signed memorandums of understanding to drill in the ITT block with various state-run oil companies, including Sinopec of China, Enap of Chile, and Petrobras of Brazil. Furthermore, Ecuador is dependent upon oil for its budget, which had a $1.5 billion deficit in 2009. Oil production has decreased in the country and in 2008 it defaulted on $3.2 billion worth of bonds from the International Monetary Fund (IMF) that it argued were "illegitimate and illegal." The government did recapitalize the bonds and bought them back at one-third of their value, which provided it with $400 million.[32] Remittances, which were also a strong source of income for the country, have dropped significantly. They were down 8.6 percent in 2008 and 22 percent in 2009.[33] President Correa refuses to accept IMF and World Bank loans to make up this budget shortfall, and has asked these institutions to leave the country. Thus, regional loans from banks such as the Inter-American Development Bank (IADB) are some of his only options in such tight financial times.

There have also been discussions between the Ecuadorian and Chinese governments for a $1 billion loan in return for oil sales to China. This loan would be a down payment for 96,000 barrels of oil a day at the day's price for twenty-four months. China has been aggressively pursuing oil in the region, including a $10 billion line of credit to Brazil's Petrobras and $4 billion of financing to Venezuelan oil company PDVSA.[34] Given the government's previous negotiations for possible contracting of the ITT block, in addition to its dwindling coffers and lines of credit, some analysts speculate that the government may be planning to exploit the ITT block, or one part of it, with the Chinese state-run oil company.

The Yasuní Fund leaders and supporters say that this is unlikely, however, for three reasons: 1) the constitution prohibits such drilling without National Assembly consent, which they argue would be unlikely; 2) national and international civil society support for the Yasuní Fund is so high that protest would likely ensue and stop any action, as evidenced by a 2009 survey that 73 percent of Ecuadorians supported keeping oil underground;[35] and 3) most importantly, the UNDP Yasuní Fund outlines clear oversight and governance mechanisms that ensure funding reimbursement to contributors in the event of oil extraction. Alberto Acosta contends that "this is an opportunity for Ecuador and the entire world to find creative, audacious, revolutionary responses."[36]

Aside from the Yasuní Fund, Acosta contends that a separate international panel should also be created to monitor investments and project development to ensure that no monies are invested in other extractive industries, such as mining.[37] In the event that oil is extracted from ITT, the state will lose the fund, which must be returned to donors.[38] Theoretically, then, those who donate to the Yasuní-ITT Initiative essentially self-guarantee; the more money given by the world, the less likely the government is to drill, as funds should be more than comparable to profits earned from oil extraction. As funds accumulate, it is less likely that the government would desire to return funding and exploit the area, thus creating another form of global co-responsibility.

Technical glitches have surfaced. First, Executive Decree 847 from January 2008, which created the Government Coordinating Entity of the Yasuní Fund, only provides for donor reimbursement in the case of oil extraction for sums above \$20,000. The August 3, 2010, UNDP agreement with Ecuador states that the Steering Committee will set the minimum threshold for reimbursement. However, it is not likely that individuals and/or small organizations will donate in sums above this amount. Therefore, the steering committee will have to reformulate its contract with the international society if it would like to encourage individual contributions, or even those from foundations and international organizations.

Additionally, the same decree gives the right for the trust fund to invest in the Ecuadorian government. This implies that the government can use funds for its own purposes, beyond those of the National Development Plan or Yasuní Park protection. Climate Focus has suggested that this area be stricken from the decree as it creates a conflict of interest. It further suggests that the government formulate a policy manual for board operations, which would include other areas of conflict of interest, such as nepotism policies and investments in board member–related projects and/or programs. Lastly, it recommends that the Steering Committee and the Government Coordinating Entity be expanded to include non-voting members who have experience in the area and that oversight committees composed of experts for various sectors of project implementation and evaluation be formed.[39] These areas of concern will need to be addressed by the yet-to-be-announced members of the Yasuní Fund Steering Committee.

International support resides not only with leading environmental NGOs nationally and internationally, but also among international scholars, statesmen, and Nobel Prize winners. They include Nobel Prize winners Archbishop Desmond Tutu and Rigoberta Menchú, as well as political leaders Mikhail Gorbachev and Felipe González, among others. The German Parliament, the Organization of American States (OAS), OPEC, the UNDP, the IUCN, and the Andean Community of Nations all support the initiative as well. Neighboring Bolivian leader, Evo Morales, has also announced his country's desire to possibly replicate the initiative. Thus, international momentum and support is backing the initiative.[40]

Global precedent, however, is lacking. Other trust funds of such magnitude do not exist. First, the Yasuní-ITT Initiative is globally unique. Its point is to change current thinking on climate change policy and break new ground. Second, other environmental trust funds, such as those in the World Bank, have funds of up to approximately \$800 million. The amount of money for the Yasuní-ITT Fund should eventually rise over \$350 million per year for ten years, totaling \$4.55 billion, not including accrued interest and estimated potential gains from CDM and REDD-related projects (if they are eventually included in the funding options). Thus, careful scrutiny and implementation of this pilot plan is highly recommended so that, as Ecuador suggests, other megadiverse countries may replicate it.

Replication, Megadiversity, and Saving the Amazon

Concerns persist about replication. Some fear that wealthy oil-exporting countries, like Saudi Arabia, may try to join such initiatives if accepted as part of a post-Kyoto accord. Among other issues, analysts fear such a policy could increase oil prices and/or pay oil exporters higher prices, in addition to increasing reserves for future development. However, Ecuadorian officials argue that their approach avoids these problems by limiting the applicability to:

- Developing countries. One of this mechanism's main attractions is that it simultaneously fulfills three objectives: it combats climate change, maintains biodiversity, and reduces poverty and inequality. The initiative also promotes sustainable development.
- Megadiverse countries located between the Tropics of Cancer and Capricorn, where tropical forests are concentrated. These countries host most of the planet's biodiversity.
- Countries that have significant fossil fuel reserves in highly biologically and culturally sensitive areas.

Among the countries satisfying all of these conditions are Brazil, Colombia, Costa Rica, the Democratic Republic of Congo, Ecuador, India, Indonesia, Madagascar, Malaysia, Papua Nueva Guinea, Peru, Bolivia, the Philippines, and Venezuela. Therefore, it would exclude countries like China, Russia, and the US and would avoid an excessive supply of similar projects.[41]

Even though the evidence of destruction and declining oil reserves in the Amazon persists, initiatives continue to build roads and extract natural resources. An example is the Initiative for Regional Infrastructure Integration (IIRSA). One plan on the drawing board directly impacts the Amazon: the Manta-Manaus project. In September 2008, President Correa and project coordinators in Ecuador went to Singapore to seek funding to build a transportation system of roads and waterways that would traverse the Amazonian region, beginning in the Brazilian Amazonian city of Manaus and terminating at the Ecuadorian Pacific port-city of Manta.[42] Researchers like Dr. David Romo of La Universidad San Francisco de Quito and the Tiputini Biosphere Reserve in Ecuador's Amazon are confounded by such disparate policies in the same region.[43] While REDD initiatives may abate this level of deforestation, coordination of policies across Amazonian countries is needed.

One sign of hope in this area is the Amazon Cooperation Treaty Organization (OTCA). It was founded in 1978 by the eight Amazonian countries

(Brazil, Guyana, Suriname, Ecuador, Peru, Colombia, Venezuela, and Bolivia) and was formalized with a governing headquarters in Brasilia in 1995. In November 2009, the organization hosted a conference in Brazil on indigenous peoples and their territories with the goal of outlining common policies to protect them.[44] However, the organization is weak and lacks authority within the member nations. Supporters of the Yasuní-ITT proposal have called upon member nations to support the proposal and strengthen it by replication throughout the region. So far, Brazil has created the Amazon Fund, to which Norway has donated $1 billion, to prevent deforestation. Yet, no serious discussions of coordination to resist natural resources extraction and develop a common policy in this area have emerged. A possible block of Amazonian countries, led by Ecuador and Brazil, to support unique initiatives like that of Yasuní-ITT might create a political force within UNFCCC negotiations. The problems, however, are the conflicts of interest over oil exploration in this resource-rich area and lack of general state interest to leave it underground.

From Quito to Cancun, and Beyond?

The key elements of the Yasuní-ITT Initiative intertwine local and global issues, from reduced carbon emissions and the protection of biodiversity and human rights to poverty and inequality reduction. Each Ecuadorian goal parallels the international agreements on global climate change, the Convention on Biological Diversity, the IAHCR ruling to protect uncontacted indigenous peoples, and the Millennium Development Goals aimed at fighting poverty and inequality. As technical adviser Carlos Larrea recently pointed out at a conference updating the Ecuadorian public on the proposal, the initiative benefits Ecuadorian people directly, as their near forty-year experience with petroleum extraction has left them as one of the poorest countries in Latin America in terms of economic development; over 50 percent of its population lives at or below the poverty level. Thus, he observed, petro-dollars were not the windfall for economic "takeoff" that Ecuadorians had hoped for since the 1970s. Additionally, Ecuador's oil supply, while it peaked at over 500,000 barrels in 2000, is diminishing. Like it or not, Ecuador will become an oil importer in the next thirty years or so, if it does not develop an alternate path for energy and sustainable livelihood.[45] This scenario is, unfortunately, a familiar one among other megadiverse developing nations.

The Yasuní-ITT plan highlights some of the Kyoto Protocol weaknesses and seeks to improve them for the developing world through normative and structural changes. The key ingredients are the people who have collectively mobilized to create this proposal over a number of years. The first weakness that the proposal addresses is normative: leaving fossil fuels underground, or unused—avoided emissions, instead of emissions absorption and/or reduction. This normative change is significant to developing countries, which are estimated to feel the brunt of global warming, most particularly the Amazon and its watersheds that are threatened with drying out. This change is a profound one in that it seeks to change the lifestyle of global citizens by encouraging their societies to avoid carbon emissions, rather than compensate for them. It also aligns with the concept of *buen vivir*, or living a lifestyle within nature, rather than dominating it, and protecting it for future generations.

The second weakness that this proposal addresses is the issue of ecological debt, which was highlighted in the Rio discussions in 1992, but never realized in any concrete manner.[46] Ecuador, however, has changed the normative underpinnings of ecological debt to co-responsibility and shared compensation between Ecuador and the international community. The goal is to stop pointing fingers and establish lasting sustainable change for peoples and their environment on local and global levels.

The third weakness that is addressed is the direction: from Annex 1 to Annex 0, which means the developing world wants a say in its global environment and the policies that protect it and its citizens. Ecuador's new constitution (2008) not only gives rights to nature and protects uncontacted peoples, but it outlines new politics of the good life. Alberto Acosta explains that the good life is a concept that is not just Ecuadorian, but can be applied globally to all societies, as it seeks dialog among peoples and their governments to create sustainable living conditions and an economy that reflects the values of societies, over the value of material goods. US scholars Herman Daly, Thomas Princen, Ken Conca, Michael Maniates, and James Gustave Speth, among others advocate similar normative changes toward economies that include nature, rather than those that make it an externality.

This proposal is unique in that it potentially includes other global proposals that were discussed at the 2010 Cancun UNFCCC conference, such as REDD, in addition to both social and "avoided emissions" elements. Furthermore, the contention is to permit Ecuador to be a pilot case for the world, sacrificing one of its largest oil reserves, to then help replicate the plan in other megadiverse areas of the planet. It also potentially includes elements of CDM from the Kyoto Protocol, which emphasizes a willingness to work within currently accepted international norms, but to also push them beyond their limits with new concepts. These new concepts will be materialized in new global governance structures through the Yasuní Fund and its steering committee, the UNDP oversight of the trust fund, and possible new forms of carbon trade, debt for CGY swaps, and individual contributions.

Finally, some may ask: Why pay to keep oil underground, if extraction is cost prohibitive? The answer to that question is twofold: 1) there has already been interest from China, Chile, Brazil, and from other oil companies to drill in Yasuní and there is currently drilling within the park; 2) it is worth it to protect the planet's most biodiverse region for its value for recreation, bioprospecting, watershed services, and mere existence. The answer from Ecuador would likely be: for the good life. People cannot maintain the rapid pace of industrialization without considering the implications for the health of the Earth. While the good life may seem utopian, like many norms, it is a goal. Ecuador prefers to seek the good life before the Amazon turns to savannah and the solutions looked at for 2012 and beyond pale compared to the dismal reality of a planet in ruins.

Notes

1. Pamela Martin, "Ecuador's Biodiverse Paradise Could Still Be Lost to Oil," *Environmental News Service*, February 16, 2010, http://www.ens-newswire.com/ens/feb2010/2010-02-16-02.html.

2. Ibid.

3. Carlos Larrea, "Resumen expo COICA," http://www.youtube.com/watch?v=tqRCOiZTfNo.

4. Article 407 and 408 refer directly to this initiative and to the state's inalienable rights to non-renewable natural resources.

5. Joseph Henry Vogel, *The Economics of the Yasuní Initiative: Climate Change as if Thermodynamics Mattered* (London: Anthem Press, 2009), 61.

6. "United Nations Human Development Index 2010 Rankings," United Nations Development Program, http://hdr.undp.org/en/statistics/.

7. Carlos Larrea et al.,"Yasuní-ITT Initiative a Big Idea from a Small Country," Yasuní ITT Initiative official website, July 2009, http://www.yasuni-itt.gov.ec/download/Yasuni_ITT_Initiative1009.pdf, 12.

8. "Alemania dispuesta a contribuir al ITT-Yasuní," *El Comercio*, June 6, 2009 (translation by author).

9. Alberto Acosta et al., "A Political, Economic, and Ecological Initiative in the Ecuadorian Amazon," Americas Program Policy Report, accessed July 30, 2010, http://americas.irc-online.org/am/6345; Matthieu Le Quang, "La moratoria petrolífera en la Amazonía ecuatoriana, una propuesta inspiradora para la Cumbre de Copenhague," *Boletín ECOS* 8 (September 10, 2009): 1–23.

10. "Alemania dispuesta a contribuir al ITT-Yasuní," *El Comercio*, June 6, 2009 (translation by author).

11. Dr. Francisco Carrión (Ecuadorian ambassador to the United Nations), telephone interview, August 19, 2010.

12. "Ecuador Yasuní ITT Trust Fund: Terms of Reference," *National Government of Ecuador and United Nations Development Programme*, 5-8, http://mdtf.undp.org/document/search?fund=3EY00&document_areas=fund,project&go=true.

13. Vogel, *Economics of the Yasuní Initiative*, 68–69.

14. See also Sven Wunder, *The Economics of Deforestation: The Example of Ecuador* (Basingstoke, UK: Macmillan Press, 2000) for a detailed discussion of deforestation in Ecuador.

15. Larrea et al., "Yasuní-ITT Initiative," 18. These figures are based on the value of $17.66 per metric ton of carbon.

16. Fander Falconí and Carlos Larrea, "Impactos ambientales de las políticas de liberalización externa y los flujos de capital: el caso de Ecuador," In *Globalización y Desarrollo en América Latina* ed. Fander Falconí, Marcelo Hercowitz, and Roldan Muradian (Quito, Ecuador: FLACSO, 2004).

17. Larrea et al. "Yasuní-ITT Initiative," 16. Silvestrum consulting firm was contracted by the Ecuadorian government, via funding from the German government's international cooperation enterprise, Deutsche Gesellschaft für Technische Zusammenarbeit (GTZ). The figures cited here are from their 2009 report.

18. Acosta et al., "Political, Economic, and Ecological Initiative."

19. From Le Quang, "La moratoria petrolífera en la Amazonía ecuatoriana," 1–23 (translation by author).

20. Alberto Acosta, interview, Quito, Ecuador, February 27, 2009; author translation from the Spanish: "*Pero lo que nosotros estamos pensando es de Kyoto a Quito. Esa es la idea nuestra, dar un salto, el ITT abre una visión diferente.*"

21. Decreto Ejecutivo 847, 3.

22. "Análisis Legal y Financiero de la Implementación de la Iniciativa ITT-Yasuní," Climate Focus, 2009, http://www.yasuni-itt.gov.ec/download/Reporte_Legal_Climate_Focus.pdf. "Los Certificados de Garantía Yasuní y el Fideicomiso Mercantil de Transformación Energética," *Corporación Financiera Nacional*, (January 9, 2008), 29.

23. Decreto Ejecutivo 847, 2; José Vicente Troya, interview, Quito, Ecuador, February 18, 2009.

24. Decreto Ejecutivo 847, 2.

25. Decreto Ejecutivo 1572, 2; budget information per interview with Natalia Greene, Quito, Ecuador, February 12, 2009.

26. Decreto Ejecutivo 1572, 1.

27. Decreto Ejecutivo 882, 2.

28. Esperanza Martínez, "Dejar El Crudo en Tierra en el Yasuní—Un Reto a la Coherencia," *Revista Tendencia* 9 (April 2009): 1–13.

29. Vogel, *Economics of the Yasuní Initiative*, 20.

30. Acosta, interview, Quito, Ecuador, February 27, 2009.

31. "Ecuador Yasuní-ITT Trust Fund: Terms of Reference," 14–15.

32. "Ecuador, Argentina and the IMF: The Price of Pride," *Economist*, September 10, 2009.

33. "Ecuador Remittances Fall 21 pct in First 6 Months," Forbes.com, http://www
.forbes.com/feeds/ap/2009/08/17/ap6787416.html (accessed October, 25 2009).

34. Eduardo García, "Ecuador Mulls 2-Year Oil Supply Deal with China," Reuters,
July 20, 2009.

35. "Mesa redonda en la FLACSO," Iniciativa Yasuní-ITT, http://www.yasuni-itt
.gov.ec/contenidos.asp?id_page=76.

36. Le Quang, "La moratoria petrolífera en la Amazonía ecuatoriana," 16.

37. Ibid.

38. Larrea et al., "Yasuní-ITT Initiative," 25–26.

39. "Análisis Legal y Financiero de la Implementación de la Iniciativa ITT-Yasuní,"
Climate Focus, 25–28.

40. Iniciativa Yasuní-ITT, "Apoyo Internacional Recibido," http://www.llacta.org/
notic/2007/not0524c.htm (accessed November 15, 2009).

41. Larrea et al., "Yasuní-ITT Initiative." Joseph Henry Vogel's critique of the
Yasuní-ITT Initiative is that it needs to include carbon-rich and economically poor
countries, rather than the geographical delineations suggested by the Ecuadorian
government's technical team.

42. "Correa aboga por carretera Manta-Manaos," *El Universo*, September 30, 2009.

43. David Romo, interview, Quito, Ecuador, March 25, 2009.

44. "Declaración de los Jefes de Estado sobre la Organización," Organización de
Tratado de Cooperación Amazónica, http://www.otca.org.br/publicacao/SPT-TCA
-ECU-20.pdf.

45. "Mesa redonda en la FLACSO," Iniciativa Yasuní-ITT, http://www.yasuni-itt
.gov.ec/contenidos.asp?id_page=76.

46. J. Martínez Alier, "El rol de la economía ecológica en América Latina," in *Globalización y Desarrollo en América Latina*, ed. Fander Falconí, Marcelo Hercowitz, and
Roldan Muradian (Quito, Ecuador: FLACSO, 2004).

5

Behind the Scenes

Agents, Norms, and Structure in the Quest to Save Yasuní

A N ECONOMIC EXPLANATION for the Yasuní-ITT proposal is that payment of $350 million a year for ten years benefits Ecuador more than the revenues and environmental values forgone by leaving the oil underground. However, this would explain only a small aspect of the larger dynamics among the actors involved in the campaign since its inception. These actors describe a new conceptualization of the planet, their country, and its energy matrix. They reveal the complex interpersonal negotiations and institutional change that have culminated in one of Ecuador's premier foreign policies and a possible alternative for megadiverse countries with fossil fuels. The project is being spearheaded by Ecuador's own president, Rafael Correa, who has presented the plan in person to various international audiences, including on an international tour in Europe where he spoke in London and Brussels, visited with heads of state, and made a presentation to OPEC and to the United Nations Climate Change Conference in Cancun, Mexico.

The discourse of government officials, NGO representatives, and transnational and state-based oil company representatives lends itself to political analysis. Through a series of detailed interviews, I attempt to extract not only the story behind this groundbreaking proposal, but also the motivations of the actors and expectations for success or failure. Their words may reveal not just the motivations, but also the normative underpinnings of the campaign and the structural changes that take place when new ideas replace longtime institutionalized norms and government structures. While the reader may first assume that transnational oil company and state-based Petroecuador representatives would not think twice about drilling in the country's largest reserve, such characterization is not accurate; which leads to another question: Is President Correa presenting this plan to the world in a show of "green" leadership? Or are these reserves so difficult to access and so expensive to develop and transport the heavy crude that the Yasuní option may be his only option? While legitimate questions and concerns, the analysis to follow will reveal that the answers to these questions lies in the complex web of transnational networks that impact such policy outcomes.

There is another aspect of this analysis that is rarely examined by social scientists, but nevertheless is quite significant. Belief in an idea like this seems to be contagious. In fact, President Correa remarked that "Roque Sevilla's [former CAD president] enthusiasm for this proposal is contagious."[1] The structures that would support the implementation of this proposal, as demonstrated in the previous chapter, do not yet exist. The markets to sell avoided carbon emissions do not exist. Yet, actors involved in this campaign are convinced that they can alter the structural processes and create not just a post-Kyoto scheme for the world community, but an entirely different way to view sustainable development. Such is the "leap." As demonstrated below, this state policy did not come to fruition without struggle and it still faces an upward climb as leaders seek its funding worldwide.

While some may refer to her as radical, others describe her as tenacious or outspoken. In any event, Esperanza Martínez, director of Oilwatch International and founding member of Acción Ecológica, a Quito-based environmental NGO, is one of the founders of the Yasuní-ITT proposal and one of its most outspoken proponents. Going to an interview at Acción, near La Universidad Central in Quito, is an experience in community living: members are playing soccer, drinking coffee, and constantly whirling around the office discussing campaigns and the latest strategies. The energy level is high as members text message, e-mail, and talk on the phone with others in the field or at the government agencies. Oftentimes, indigenous community members turn up to discuss new policies and strategies. The offices are brightly colored, although certainly not ultra-modern or ornate, with a large, welcoming garden courtyard. The first time I spoke with Esperanza about this initiative was in 2006, facing this garden. I have spoken with Esperanza over a period of thirteen years and her determination to save the Amazon and place a moratorium against petroleum development in her country has not changed. She whisks through her office with a cup of coffee, amid her multitasking of Skype voice over Internet protocol (VOIP) conversations, e-mails, and conversations with other Acción members.

When asked what international norms she thinks the Yasuní-ITT proposal is based on, she responded: "I think that there is a combination . . . the climate change norms and those that apply to biodiversity, and eventually those that apply to indigenous peoples; those are the international norms. The three are important tools."[2] For Martínez and others in the campaign, international norms are building blocks, or "tools," on which the campaign is based in the global community. They immediately recognize the global structures on which the proposal is based.

Yet global norms are only part of the foundation of the proposal to keep oil underground in Yasuní. Martínez sums up the initial phase of the campaign in the following manner:

> The antecedents to the proposal I find in a series of discussions that we had in Ecuador various years ago, maybe ten years ago, in which Alberto Acosta was a part. They spoke about the need for a post-petroleum Ecuador. From them, various struggles for resistance began in Ecuador and in other parts of the world. This vindicates the fact that there are local peoples who do not want petroleum and have the right to a distinct model. Finally, a petition, which also has a story of some years, to propose moratoriums on the opening of the petroleum zone, and in Ecuador there has been a moratorium de facto in many zones, all the southern part of the Amazonía. Somehow, the sum of these three facts, the horizon of the post-petroleum Ecuador, the moratorium, when the expectation to exploit Yasuní was launched, the designing of a proposal for this zone started to be discussed.[3]

Here we note the process of alternative international norm creation in which a "distinct model" of development is established from the perspective of local communities—Ecuador *post-petrolero*. This model, according to Martínez and others, originated through a series of struggles in other areas of the Amazon and in other petroleum-exporting developing countries, a fact that demonstrates the possibility of social learning among communities. In the process of institutionalizing the new post-petroleum norm, political opportunity structures (POS) in the form of government planning in the ITT zone on oil extraction and the key social actor, Alberto Acosta—formerly associated with Acción Ecológica and minister of energy and mines in 2007—created catalysts for future structural and policy changes within the government.

Martínez and her colleagues from Oilwatch formed a technical team of biologists, geologists, and other scientists to respond to the government studies of ITT petroleum extraction and provide sound reasons not to develop it. As the viability of the plan to leave crude oil underground became more convincing, Alberto Acosta was nominated as minister of energy and mines. When asked if Acosta, who is a friend of President Correa, was appointed to this position to promote this alternative policy of Ecuador *post-petrolero*, he responded, "It was by chance. It is a coincidence."[4]

Alberto Acosta is one of the most respected contemporary political thinkers in Ecuador. He is currently a professor at the Facultad Latinamericana de

Ciencias Sociales (FLACSO) in Quito and was the director of the Constituent Assembly to rewrite Ecuador's constitution in 2008, in addition to being minister of energy and mines. His writings include works on the new constitution, globalization and the Amazon, the concept of the good life, and an economic history of the country. Acosta studied in Cologne, Germany, and holds a doctorate in energy economics, which explains his experience in energy issues and his networks promoting the campaign with the German government.

A conversation with him reveals his deep concern for the Amazon and his commitment to Ecuador *post-petrolero* and the Yasuní-ITT proposal. In addition, Acosta emphasized his personal relationship to the Amazon. He explained:

> I was coming from a personal process of great connection to the oil sector and to the Amazonía, in particular. I was in the Amazonía for the first time during the mid-50s, and then I had great romantic connection with the Amazonía because I used to travel, to stroll, to travel on the motorboat, to walk; I was in many places. I like the Amazonía a lot. Then, I was in the Amazonía as a petroleum employee; I worked for the state petroleum company and had this narrow vision of "a *petrolero*" ["an oil man"]. We had to extract more and more oil. I was the company's marketing manager. Therefore, I had to extract oil, send oil, and when there were problems I had to go and see what was going on. I had another vision. Later I was the minister.[5]

Acosta later revealed that his uncle was president José María Velasco Ibarra, who first began oil extraction in the northern Amazon with Texaco. He accompanied his uncle in his youth on trips to this sector, including the inauguration of the Texaco block where the company brought an entire banquet from Quito via helicopter to Lago Agrio, including dry ice sculptures. He remembered being dazzled by what they thought at the time was modernization. Now, he relayed, he understands how sadly mistaken they were.[6] The personal relationship that an actor has with the proposal is another key ingredient in the social learning process and in the networking process. Acosta's networks have facilitated key contacts in Germany, which has provided the most substantial research funding for the project. Finally, his personal experiences have created an identification with the Amazonian region, which according to him, has inspired his action and dedication to the Yasuní-ITT Initiative.

While many have called Acosta "the father of the Yasuní-ITT Initiative" or "the brain behind the proposal," Acosta brushes aside these claims and says instead:

> This is a collective initiative in a strict sense. If I was the one who had to present it publicly for the first time, it does not mean I am the author, nor the

father of the initiative. I do not deny my commitment to the initiative, but I cannot assume a paternity that I do not have or own. This is the result, on one side, of various studies, works, investigations that have been made in Ecuador about the oil.

Many years ago, Acción Ecológica sponsored a study called "Post-petroleum Ecuador" that was published. . . . It arises from this source; it arises also from the reality in Amazonía, from all the indigenous peoples, settlers, peasants' resistance who also presented a lawsuit against Texaco. Therefore, there is a claim felt throughout the region that also feeds the struggle for a more responsible management in the oil sector, not only the reparations from all the damage caused by Chevron-Texaco, but a different management, more serious, more committed to human beings and nature.[7]

Yet other actors involved in aspects of the Yasuní-ITT block perceive Alberto Acosta's involvement differently. First, people politics are at play; all interviewees mention Acosta's name as one key element in the takeoff of the initiative. However, the perception of Acosta's involvement is different depending on the position of the actor. One multinational oil company representative, who wished to remain unnamed, said that

the ITT initiative, which I think is a great idea, comes from Alberto Acosta, more than from even Fander [Fander Falconí, minister of foreign affairs], because Alberto has always been an ecologist at heart. Alberto should not have been minister of energy, but minister of environment. And he is married to an environmentalist. If these are the realities, what we will see more in Ecuador and in the world, is that we should be responsible for the things we do.[8]

This statement reveals yet another aspect of the local-global connection in policy making, particularly in oil-dependent countries. There is an intense inter-institutional competition between ministries—in this case, the Ministry of Energy and Mines (now called Non-renewable Resources) and the Ministry of the Environment. This interviewee, like others in the petroleum area with whom I spoke, criticized the placement of an environmentally-minded minister of energy and mines. Yet, this person also recognized that policies in Ecuador and globally are changing; in other words, all companies must be environmentally responsible. Still, structures are embedded and new norms that usher in new institutions take time to implement. This long-term approach has been emphasized many times by President Rafael Correa, who has argued that the path to "the good life" is long-term societal and global change.[9]

Carlos Larrea, technical advisor to the proposal and professor at La Universidad Andina Simón Bolívar, corroborated Alberto Acosta's key role in the inception of the initiative as a link between the government and civil society. He also cited President Correa as a catalyst because the president was a professor of environmental economics at La Universidad San Francisco de Quito, which Larrea contends "was important. The president decided [to approve the initiative], which created a totally new scenario and so began the project officially."[10] Larrea, who worked with Acosta and Martínez on the Acción Ecológica book entitled *Ecuador Post Petrolero*, understands the social networks between civil society and the government, and their influences. Larrea and Minister of Foreign Affairs Fander Falconí also published an article together on the devastating impacts of the petroleum industry on Ecuador's economic growth.[11]

At the global level, Larrea notes three important converging variables on the initiation of the Yasuní-ITT proposal: 1) the Nobel Prize to former US vice president Al Gore and the Intergovernmental Panel on Climate Change (IPCC) in 2007; 2) *The Stern Review on the Economics of Climate Change*[12]; and 3) President Correa's speech to the United Nations on climate change and Ecuador's work through the UN system for this project. According to Larrea, these international factors have intensified global concerns about climate change and facilitated a global consciousness on the issue. Thus, Ecuador could seize the political opportunity at the global level to gain support for its proposal.[13]

Larrea's observations corroborate with news and media accounts that

> from the moment when the news appeared of the decision by the board of directors of Petroecuador about ITT, with the backing of the energy minister [Alberto Acosta] who had originally proposed the idea, news of the plan spread like wildfire. Then institutions such as the WRI [World Resources Institute] came in; Alberto Acosta did a videoconference with them.[14]

The international campaign began with a videoconference in May 2007 to the World Wildlife Fund (WWF) office and several other INGOs, including WRI and Save America's Forests, in Washington, D.C., in collaboration with University of Maryland. Save America's Forests brought three Waorani leaders to the WWF office for the videoconference, and one of them, Fernando Nihua, vice president of the Waorani organization ONHAE, spoke for ten minutes on camera in support of the Yasuní-ITT Initiative immediately after Alberto Acosta spoke.[15] Following the international videoconference, in June 2007, President Correa officially launched the plan from the Presidential Palace.[16] The transnational network for the Yasuní-ITT campaign appeared immediately and one tool for such strategy was videoconference, a technology that has been used various times throughout the campaign. This is new and unique to transnational networks, as it has been only the last few years in which reliable videoconference connections have been available from Ecuador.

Skype VOIP conferences have also been utilized for meetings and strategy sessions. Acción Ecológica has parties interested in the Yasuní-ITT campaign on an e-mail listserv. When an issue of importance arises that leaders feel members need to discuss, it calls a *minga*—a group/community endeavor in the Quichua language whose cultural equivalent for the American would be an Amish barn-raising. At one *minga* in its office in Quito, I observed members gather to discuss their thoughts on the addition of carbon market trading to the proposal. This meeting was conducted via Skype VOIP for international members to hear and comment. WRI has also hosted a few teleconference meetings about the proposal. Participants frequently use this technology and increasingly rely on it for transnational network organization, mobilization, strategizing, and daily communication and information-sharing among members.

While the initiative seemed to gain momentum in the summer of 2007, it quickly lost its pace in the fall of 2007 as institutional conflicts began to arise. One of the strongest criticisms of the proposal was that it was not supported institutionally within the Correa government. Various members of civil society, including NGOs and IGOs, commented that President Correa never created a "home" for the initiative and kept moving its institutional base and leadership, which concerned them. It created a sense of instability and gave the perception of a lack of support on behalf of the government, according to some interviewees. Esperanza Martínez summed up the institutional "ping pong" like this:

> The proposal was born without a place. First, this was because it was presented by the minister of energy and mines. Since Alberto's departure from the ministry, it was divided in two, one of energy and other of mines and oil, and Alberto left to be a candidate to the Assembly. Therefore, the proposal moved to the [office of the] vice-presidency. From the vice-presidency some signals were given, a visit to Yasuní was organized, some letters about "Vive Yasuní" were circulated around the world, a web page was opened, a process was started, but it was a process with a lot of weaknesses because it did not have a technical team. After the vice-presidency, where the proposal did not develop, it went to the Ministry of Foreign Affairs. At the beginning there was no one at the ministry responsible for the proposal beyond the minister herself and some of her assistants, such as Lucía Gallardo. There were various activities, but nothing very organized. Perhaps the most coherent activity carried out by the ministry was this meeting in the United States, where the WRI and Max Christian's group intervened.[17]

Federico Starnfeld, a German International Cooperation (GIZ) advisor,[18] commented in our interview that

> There are plenty of groups, there is a huge complexity in those groups and each one has a different level of information. I say that the institutional subject, the political subject, is what is going to make this initiative fail or succeed.

The technical details are not very important, because I have seen that it has generated so much impact at the international level.[19]

These discourses are echoed in hundreds of conversations on this initiative, formal and informal, over the years. Furthermore, they point to the anchoring factor in policy making on the local and global levels: domestic politics matter. Even though there has always been enormous international acceptance by INGOs, IGOs, and collaborating states on this initiative, its institutional weaknesses have prevented it from going forward. For that reason, President Correa and his CAD representatives are conducting international meetings to explain the structural features that have now been created, including financial management by the UNDP, the CAD institutionalization within the Correa government (the Government Coordinating Entity within the Yasuní-ITT Trust Fund), and the National Development Plan.

SENPLADES—the National Secretariat of Planning and Development—is a key institutional instrument for change within the country. One outcome of the creation of new, alternative domestic norms in Ecuador was the National Development Plan. The former Minister of Foreign Affairs Fander Falconí was also the previous director of SENPLADES. He, therefore, is well aware of the implementation of new norms within Ecuadorian society, such as post-petroleum policies like Yasuní-ITT. Falconí, trained as an ecological economist, has spoken widely both nationally and internationally about the Yasuní-ITT proposal and wrote about a post-petroleum Ecuador as a researcher before his tenure in government. Carlos Larrea commented that Falconí's involvement in the initiative "gave important political weight to the initiative."[20] Alberto Acosta agrees that the SENPLADES national plan "generated the conditions" institutionally that supported the new post-petroleum norms outlined in the Yasuní-ITT proposal.[21]

How Did They Get There?

Roque Sevilla in February 2009 confidently defended the Yasuní-ITT plan in a phone conversation and related the strong desire to launch a new strategy, not just for Ecuador, but for the world. Sevilla negated the criticisms that called the proposal "romanticism," and said that the CAD would work hard to make the initiative a reality.[22] Watching Sevilla later in March at the CAD workshop to examine consultant reports, it was clear that his enthusiasm had only grown. He and his colleague, Yolanda Kakabadse, led a lively conversation on how to "think outside the box" to create a truly innovative global strategy to keep oil underground in pristine parts of the developing world. Throughout his time as CAD president, Sevilla commented that he became involved in the initiative because he believes in its tenets and wants to improve the planet for future generations. These statements were supported by his choice to continue his service in the CAD in 2009 over running for political office.

Yolanda Kakabadse, former minister of the environment and longtime member of the environmental NGO community, including World Resources Institute (WRI), has been a venerable force for the campaign from civil society. Kakabadse commented in an interview that she had known of the proposal a year before her tenure in the CAD from a meeting that Alberto Acosta had called with previous ministers of the environment in which he asked for their ideas and their support. Kakabadse says that she accepted the president's appointment to the CAD because of her work in Yasuní when she was minister of the environment. She said, "When I was minister I had declared the *zona intangible* in Yasuní and Cuyabeno; therefore, Yasuní is especially important to me."[23]

While Roque Sevilla and Yolanda Kakabadse, both formerly of Fundación Natura—an Ecuadorian environmental NGO—were likely candidates for the Yasuní-ITT CAD, the third member of the group, Francisco Carrión, was somewhat of an outlier. His diplomatic experience, having been minister of foreign affairs, demonstrates the reason for his selection. Carrión's role has been to market the plan internationally. Under his tutelage, many international celebrities, scholars, and leaders have given their public approval of the proposal. Carrión, however, had his doubts about such a unique plan at the global level when he was first asked by President Correa to be on the CAD team. Carrión commented:

> I was skeptical at the beginning because for me it is fundamental that such a bold, original proposal must have extremely consistent and strong political support so it can be transformed to a state policy. Therefore, I said "I want to talk to the president to see if we are on the same wavelength. If I am going to represent him, I want to know how he thinks. And, I would like him to hear how I think to see if I am a good representative for him.[24]

Carrión expressed his concerns to President Correa about the divisions he had seen within the president's cabinet regarding the Yasuní-ITT proposal. He questioned the contrasts between the Ministries of Energy and Mines and the Environment, for example. He told the president that incoherent policies would be difficult to represent at the international level and, likely, would be unsuccessful. Carrión said that President Correa agreed with him, and that he was confident after this meeting that the president supported completely the Yasuní-ITT proposal and wanted to see it be successful.[25]

For Carrión, this proposal is "the crown jewel of the country" in terms of foreign policy. From his point of view, it has the capacity to save Ecuador's rainforest and avoid carbon emissions. According to Carrión, "it can also make Ecuador appear as a green stamp country, which in terms of international negotiations . . . including trade negotiations and many more issues, could give Ecuador more political negotiating weight than it currently has." Carrión said that he is "convinced" that this will give Ecuador much more "respect" internationally.[26] He has made it, according to other press reports, his "career goal" to successfully implement the proposal as Ecuador's representative in the United Nations (appointed October 2009), where he will work to iron out details of the international trust fund with the UNDP.[27]

Conversations with the three CAD representatives and observation of government meetings might first lead to the rational conclusion that they are either fulfilling their political/career objectives, or that Ecuador's oil reserves will be diminishing in twenty to thirty years, so selling oil underground is maximizing utility. However, careful analysis of their interview transcripts reveals their interest in the proposal is driven by norms that go beyond purely economic benefits. All three confirm that post-petroleum models of development that conserve our planet for national and global reasons, plus the benefits to future generations, are the foundations of their involvement in the process. This examination aligns with Checkel's findings that neither rational choice nor constructivist models suffice to explain policy outcomes from transnational networks.[28] It is likely a combination of rational and normative bases that inform actor decision making within these global governance arenas.

IGOs and NGOs

Non-state actors have been critical components of the transnational network surrounding the Yasuní-ITT campaign. From detailed interviews, we can deduce that actor involvement from this realm is due to two factors: 1) social linkages with other actors, and 2) shared, common norms. While issues of funding and power within the transnational network were revealed, most actors involved cited their common identification with the initiative and their common understanding of the post-petroleum norm presented in the proposal. Attempts to surmise what type of non-state actor would be involved in such an initiative identify three characteristics as common threads: a) southern-based; b) concerned with environmental justice; and c) previously involved in the region or Yasuní National Park specifically. Even though larger northern INGOs, such as Conservation International, The Nature Conservancy, and World Wildlife Fund, were involved in initial conferences on the proposal, they have played very minor roles in its formation and the mobilization of the campaign. In the case of Yasuní-ITT, southern NGOs dominate the nodes of the networks as well as the dialog about post-petroleum and post-Kyoto norms and policies. This is different from previous findings in the Amazon in which transnational networks were supported by larger, northern-based NGOs.[29]

One of the most prominent members of the Yasuní-ITT transnational network is the German International Cooperation (GIZ), the German government's agency for international development. Its environmental economic advisor, Federico Starnfeld, said that its involvement in the initiative is directly related to Alberto Acosta's close relationship with Germany. Starnfeld commented that

> The German Cooperation is involved through Alberto Acosta's direct initiative. Acosta has always had a close relationship with Germany, because he studied there. He established a series of contacts while there; he worked for a German organization; his relationship with Germany is very close. Thus, one of the first countries he contacted was Germany; not directly, but through contacts here in the country [Ecuador]. I think he had a meeting with the German ambassador, who channeled his interest through to us. They held a first meeting in March 2007, in which my ex-boss participated. She was thrilled with the idea and started a series of contacts, coming and going to Germany with our central office.[30]

Starnfeld's history of the initial contacts with his office illustrates the significance of personal ties within transnational networks, in addition to committed members of the network who facilitate other opportunities.

Starnfeld's role in the initiative has been critical. While I was interviewing him, he received various phone calls from CAD president Roque Sevilla and two of the international consulting agencies working on implementation strategies. Starnfeld's participation began in March 2007, before that of the CAD members. Thus, he has a longer institutional trajectory and often explains the history of the initiative to new members of the network. Starnfeld plays a key role of *information bridge* among network members and technical consultants inside and outside of the government.[31]

As of December 2010, Federico Starnfeld's role includes supporting the Ecuadorian Ministry of the Environment to develop the REDD+ national strategy and projects. His technical transition is significant in that it illustrates Germany's commitment and support to such deforestation and degradation prevention programs. REDD+ projects, according to the Yasuní-ITT Trust Fund Terms of Reference, could also be a funding mechanism.[32] This would mean that Starnfeld's knowledge of both REDD and Socio Bosque programs (Ecuador's REDD+ initiative to prevent deforestation and degradation) and the Yasuní-ITT Trust Fund could facilitate new international collaborations and funding strategies as a model for other resource-rich developing countries. His involvement demonstrates the significance of non-state actors in a global governance process. Oftentimes, they are purveyors of information and knowledge beyond the state-based government realm and indicators of important policy changes and/or advancements.

The UNDP also has played a key role in the Yasuní-ITT transnational network as a purveyor of not only funds, but also information, social networking, and international leverage. The UNDP began its work on the Yasuní-ITT Initiative in 2008 after the Ecuadorian government, through the Ministry of the Environment, solicited UNDP support for the development of policies for leadership and conservation of Yasuní National Park. Funding was granted through a $4 million fund donated by the Spanish government toward projects relating to the Millennium Development Goals.

Specifically, the UNDP has awarded $200,000 toward the initiative to leave oil underground in the ITT block. It has researched for the Ecuadorian government four components of the plan, the publication of the proposal, and its translation. The four areas of UNDP research are: a) financial mechanisms; b) a portfolio of projects to be financed by the proposal earnings; c) national and international diffusion of the plan; and d) systematization of the experience within the UN system as a possible post-Kyoto route.[33] Manager of the UNDP office in Quito, José Vicente Troya, contends that the UNDP support for this plan is "urgent because it entails the construction of a new conceptualization of a model that stops being one of bonds and debt payment, and becomes a model based on the emission of Yasuní certificates and guarantees, which are not emitted against any kind of debt."[34]

Troya also confirmed the UNDP cooperation with the GIZ and commented that they were the two most involved intergovernmental organizations in the Yasuní-ITT Initiative. CAD president Roque Sevilla requested that the UNDP do an external review of the proposal's coherence with neoclassical economic thought, ethics, and the environment.[35] Thus, GIZ and the UNDP have had direct interaction with Ecuadorian officials and have played a hand in the design of the proposal. Furthermore, the UNDP has provided leverage for the Ecuadorian government as it seeks international support and funding for the initiative.

Aside from government officials and IGOs, non-state actors from civil society have also played critical roles in the Yasuní-ITT transnational network. Civil society created the campaign and has had varying degrees of involvement in it since the formation of the CAD in 2008. One of the precursors to the Yasuní-ITT campaign is the environmental destruction of the Northern

Amazon where the Chevron-Texaco lawsuit is now taking place. Pablo Fajardo is a local activist and one of the attorneys representing local peoples in the Chevron-Texaco case. Winner of the 2008 Goldman Environmental Prize, Pablo Fajardo also supports the Yasuní-ITT Initiative through his organization Frente de Defensa de la Amazonía and the Human Rights Committee of Shushufindi. When asked why he would support the Yasuní-ITT Initiative, Fajardo commented:

> I think it is absurd to live in a land and not get involved in what happens in the area; therefore, I have gotten involved in these types of activities because I think it is fair. I think it is the right thing to do. I think the Earth is demanding that we respect it; that we're more respectful of her; and as people we have always acted together with various social groups, indigenous, peasants, women, children, human rights supporters, environmentalists, and all the sectors that look for something fairer, more equitable, and more responsible. That is what pushes us to get involved. I think it is a just initiative that has to be carried out, it has to proceed.[36]

Fajardo's passionate response reminds us that social learning is a significant factor in why actors become involved in transnational networks. His direct experience in Lago Agrio and the Chevron-Texaco case influenced his and his organization's involvement in the campaign to save the national park to the south of their region. Furthermore, his active participation in international forums on the subject of petroleum development and human rights lends a credible voice to the Yasuní-ITT campaign. Fajardo's experience also influenced other members of the network, including Alberto Acosta, Esperanza Martínez, and Kevin Koenig (who shares office space with Fajardo).

Amazon Watch is one of the most intensely involved international NGOs in the transnational network for this campaign. Kevin Koenig, its coordinator on the ground in Ecuador, has personal linkages with Acción Ecológica since he was an intern for them in the 1990s. This, he said, was an important factor, as he earned their trust (*"confianza"*) and was therefore included in the details of the Yasuní-ITT campaign. While Koenig highlighted local knowledge as a key component of participating in this campaign, he also noted that "the internal disorganization [of the government] was shocking" in the beginning.[37] Before the CAD was institutionalized, Koenig was working with former Acción colleague, Lucía Gallardo, in the Ministry of Foreign Affairs to develop the proposal with the government. Koenig said, "It was incredible; it just underscores the fact that there was a sort of questionable commitment of the government to the proposal; when the government does a big show to announce it and then they haven't allocated staff or budget. So everybody was spending their own money, people weren't getting paid."[38]

Amazon Watch became entrenched in the Yasuní-ITT plan from the inside with the Ecuadorian government. This was a unique role for the organization, as Koenig's other job was supporting the communities involved in the lawsuit against Chevron-Texaco. This lawsuit began in the mid-1990s as a typical boomerang effect against the Ecuadorian government; the present administration now speaks out against the pollution in this region. Amazon Watch has used its international role to support Ecuador's proposal in global forums and on its website, in addition to its on-the-ground administrative and technical support to government and local NGO leaders.

The next two NGOs have both local and international offices. Their leaders are based in varying locations, as opposed to having a field officer in an international locale or working with local-partner NGOs. This aspect of their organizations provides them with direct connections on the ground in Ecuador, as well as international leverage and financial support. The Pachamama Alliance, which also houses the Ecuadorian Fundación Pachamama, has supported the Yasuní-ITT Initiative since October 2007 through technical support. The Pachamama Alliance is based in San Francisco, California, and has two fundamental goals: "1) to preserve the Earth's tropical forests by empowering indigenous people who are its natural custodians; and 2) to contribute to the creation of a new global vision of equity and sustainability for all."[39]

Natalia Greene, its representative, was a student at La Universidad Andina Simón Bolívar, where Carlos Larrea, the CAD technical advisor, was also a faculty member. Greene worked with Larrea on one of the first workshops about the initiative in November 2007, in which the international consulting firm Earth Economics of Washington, D.C., presented its economic evaluation of Yasuní National Park and the concept of environmental services in return for oil left underground. Greene noted, "At this moment Pachamama gets involved because the state made this proposal without a technical team or a budget; therefore, Pachamama finances a small consultancy in which we got involved, Carlos and I, as technicians to give the consultancy support."[40]

Greene plays a dual role as member of Pachamama Foundation and as a technical consultant for the Yasuní-ITT Initiative. She also uses her role to gain support and funding from the California-based Pachamama Alliance, headed by Bill and Lynne Twist. This aspect of combined function underscores the complexity of global governance relations in which actors oftentimes wear multiple hats in the decision-making and policy-making processes.

One of the most significant knowledge sources for the campaign has come from Finding Species and Save America's Forests, two international NGOs that focus on the scientific study of biodiversity and forests, respectively. Both of these organizations have been highly influential in terms of scientific information. Their studies and reports have been cited by the Ecuadorian government and are linked to various web pages involved in the Yasuní-ITT Initiative. Most significantly, a letter signed by fifty-nine scientists worldwide outlined the biodiversity of Yasuní National Park and its significance to the planet.[41] The scientists recommended that Ecuador enact a law prohibiting road construction and oil extraction in its national parks. This scientific data and the letter are used frequently in speeches and official government documents for the proposal.[42] In fact, an advance copy of a scientific study on biodiversity in Yasuní National Park published in early 2010 was provided to CAD officials to present in the December 2009 UNFCCC climate change talks in Copenhagen.[43] This January 2010 study is now the definitive source that is cited (by Ecuadorian government and non-governmental actors alike) for any data on biodiversity in Yasuní National Park.[44]

Finding Species began working on issues impacting the biodiversity of Yasuní National Park in 2003 when it documented, through photography, the biodiversity of the park and the effects of roads that were built for oil companies—specifically the Auca and Maxus roads within the park. In 2004, it sponsored twenty-five researchers to study Yasuní National Park and report their results in October 2004 in Mindo, Ecuador, at a conference on tropical forests. The results from this conference and the photographs combined to form a travelling photo documentary of Yasuní National Park that was displayed all over the country. The objective, according to Verónica Quitigüiña of Finding Species Ecuador, "was to raise public awareness of the diversity in Yasuní National Park."[45] Then, in 2007, when Alberto Acosta announced the plan to leave oil underground in the park's ITT block, the photographs from this exhibit were used by the Ecuadorian government in national and international meetings and conferences. Later, Finding Species aligned with Acción Ecológica and other organizations in the Acción-sponsored campaign entitled "Yasuní Depends on You."

Save America's Forests (SAF), based in Washington, D.C., has played a significant role in scientific information sharing as well. SAF scientist Dr. Matt Finer has spoken broadly on the subject and has published a number of peer-reviewed, scientific articles on the devastating impacts of oil block concessions and road construction in the Western Amazon.[46] He also wrote one of the first news reports on the initiative in April 2007, before the official campaign announcement by President Correa.[47] Additionally, he and various colleagues have published a social and political history of Yasuní National Park and its indigenous peoples.[48] Finer, who travels between Ecuador, Peru, and Washington, D.C., has been actively engaged in field research in these areas. These findings have also been cited by the Ecuadorian government and used widely on websites related to the campaign. Finer has been a strong proponent of the

PHOTO 5.1
(Left) Former minister of energy and mines Alberto Acosta (2007), live via videoconference from Ecuador. (Right) Dr. Matt Finer and assistant Ellie Happel of Save America's Forests watching the videoconference in Washington, D.C.
Source: Carl Ross, courtesy of Save America's Forests.

Yasuní-ITT proposal through his scientific investigation and collaboration with the campaign of Save America's Forests.

All three NGOs—Pachamama, Finding Species, and Save America's Forests—have provided technical support and scientific information to the transnational network. This knowledge and information have informed the proposal and the government's plan of implementation through its National Development Plan. Their role within Haas's "epistemic community"[49] has been used in creating leverage with the national government, IGOs, and other potential donors, as well as raising the consciousness of civil society about the biodiversity of the region and petroleum's negative impacts on it.

Oil Companies

While not directly involved in the Yasuní-ITT campaign, petroleum industry representatives have great authority in Ecuador given the importance of the industry in the state's budget and the political weight of the Ministry of Energy and Mines and Petroecuador. Petroleum extraction was originally the alternative, or Plan B, for the initiative. Furthermore, industry experts were consulted on the reserves and issues surrounding its extraction. Conversations with them reveal doubts about the feasibility of leaving such large reserves of oil underground. While technically a challenge, at least one industry representative admits the costs of extraction outweigh the benefits.

Former Petrobras representative, Pablo Flores, who organized the technical teams for possible development of the ITT block in 2007, described the Petrobras plan to develop the ITT block as very similar to the plan that was approved for oil extraction from Block 31, just next to ITT. Flores remarked that a form of "offshore" perforation was discussed, which "placed the treatment plant outside of the park and flew materials for the pumps via helicopter. This avoided access roads and the risks of colonization in the area."[50] Flores worked with representatives from Chile and China to develop a technical strategy for possible extraction with a clear understanding from the government that no contract or bidding was taking place.

After a detailed team analysis, Flores concluded that the ITT block "is not the crown jewel of Ecuador."[51] He argued that the issue has become "politicized, as if ITT is going to give some infinite amount of oil profit to the country."[52] In fact, his technical team estimated that an initial investment of $1.5 billion was necessary to the project and that this would require oil prices for heavy crude, or Napo, to be above $50 per barrel. Flores contended that President Correa used the possible bidding of the block as a political ploy. He commented:

> And I think it was good that he made it like that because I think he had to send a message to the ecological movement like this: perfect, here is a commercial interest proposed by these companies, you do your thing (i.e., the proposal) too; I think that perhaps that has been a motivation [for support of the Yasuní-ITT proposal].[53]

Outside of this consortium, however, Flores and other industry experts have commented that other oil operators are interested in the ITT project, most notably those from China and India.

Federico Cruz of Repsol-YPF (as of December 2010, Cruz has resigned from Repsol-YPF), a Spanish and Argentinean oil company that operates in Block 16, located in Yasuní National Park, commented:

> Surely, the government feels pressure; we do not. What we know, as is obvious, is that we operate in a difficult area. As I have explained about the relationship with the Waorani, it is a difficult situation, complicated. We do not feel the pressure because we do not have blocks 31 or ITT, but that does not mean we would not like to have them.[54]

Cruz, who was one of the founders of Fundación Natura with CAD members Roque Sevilla and Yolanda Kakabadse, argues that the Yasuní-ITT proposal is "unrealistic"; a comment echoed by his colleague and former Minister of Energy and Mines Rene Ortiz.[55]

Cruz, however, suggested an alternative plan for the country that included both the concept of carbon guarantees and oil extraction. He added, "I speak as an Ecuadorian. I see the potential behind both things. I, as Repsol, would operate with the due diligence. And the rest, I would sell as bonds through the Ecuadorian State . . . but a good business environment can be created for sure."[56]

Cruz's suggestion presents an interesting scenario for future oil development around the world. In addition to taxing barrels of oil, as discussed in previous OPEC sessions (such as the Correa-Daly tax), this idea includes extracting petroleum in environmentally sounder ways and receiving carbon credits for doing so, or leaving a part of the petroleum underground and selling avoided emissions for it. There are problems, however, with this suggestion: 1) why would someone purchase certificates for only partially avoided emissions while the area is still affected by oil extraction? 2) the norm of post-petroleum Ecuador would not be implemented; 3) aligning the mission of the certificates with the National Development Plan for alternative energies would not be included; and 4) some experts argue that low-impact oil drilling in remote, pristine areas is a myth.[57] Such a concept would also not be included in post-Kyoto guidelines for climate control, as it encourages further extractive industries in biologically sensitive areas where uncontacted populations live. Still, Cruz's idea displays the ingenuity of the oil industry in adapting to new standards and the interest in this region of the Amazon (and likely others).

Rene Ortiz, former minister of energy and mines and president of the hydrocarbons industry in Ecuador, is pessimistic about the success of the Yasuní-ITT proposal. He argues, "It is impossible that it succeeds, but impossible; although it serves their political purpose [the CAD members]."[58] Ortiz contends that Ecuador's problem is not the extractive industry per se, but rather the low technological capability of Petroecuador and the government's inability to attract competitive private investors to the country. He pointed out that Norway and Brazil have environmentally sensitive, technologically advanced state-run oil companies that Ecuador should model.[59]

While not surprising to hear an oil industry's representative touting its benefits, it is revealing to note that Ortiz, a former government leader, doubts the ability of the Ecuadorian government to collect $350 million per year to leave oil underground, rather than simply extract the oil. Ortiz's argument is based on increasing prices of heavy crude in the market as demand from emerging markets rises. While the government has said that this is a tempting argument, President Correa and the CAD have reiterated their desire not only for profit for the country, but also to create an alternative path of development for megadiverse countries that have fossil fuels. Thus, Ortiz's thesis would only be valid if the normative underpinnings of the government were to include only oil market realities, not the climate change, post-petroleum, and good life norms of its new constitution.

The petroleum industry in Ecuador agrees on one point: leaving Yasuní untouched would be the best option. When asked, most experts said that they hoped the proposal would work for the benefit of the environment and the people of the region. However, most agreed that this was improbable, as the financial crisis and rising oil prices might lead the government to develop this site. Federico Cruz contends that in the end, President Correa will tell the world and Ecuador:

> You cannot say anything. You had the chance to give the world oxygen; you had the chance to be part of the solution to the world climate problem. We have travelled around the world, you did not accept, so do not ask me more than I can do. I owe responsibility to my people. People of Ecuador, you know I have proposed, I have given the opportunity, a year, six months, but I cannot remain seated, with my people in need, without exploiting something for you, Ecuadorian people.[60]

And the Norms Behind the Proposal?
Post-petroleum, Post-Kyoto, and Human Rights

The struggle to create new norms in the international realm from below includes the processes of adaptation, bargaining, persuasion, debate, and argumentation. The Yasuní-ITT proposal is unique in that it offers innovative options for the developing world in biodiverse areas, unlike the Kyoto Protocol, which focuses on Annex 1 industrialized nations. Yet this proposal also pushes the limits because it rejects the traditional market approaches of selling unused carbon quotas or creating mitigation plans (such as the Clean Development Mechanism). Its supporters argue that it is not an add-on to Kyoto, but a mindset change from over-consumption of oil toward humans' peaceful coexistence within nature. Finally, the issue of protecting the rights of people who have communicated their desire to remain isolated is central to this proposal. While not directly related to climate change in terms of carbon emissions, it touches on a larger issue: whether market forces driven by some groups on this planet have the right to take away the homes or even possibly the existence of other groups (no matter how small their numbers may be). Are we destroying the nature and existence of some on the planet?

The sphere of acceptance of Kyoto among the actors themselves differs, as will be demonstrated. Some actors support a "Kyoto Two," which would include pilot cases like Ecuador's. On the other hand, other actors reject the

Kyoto Protocol and argue for the Yasuní-ITT proposal as a global change toward more "imaginative and creative" strategies for dealing with not only climate change, but larger issues of social justice, human dignity, and humankind's role within the environment.[61] Thus, actors involved in the initiative all support some type of alternative norm, but their level of criticism of the Kyoto Protocol differs.

Of those who support a more radical change for environmental politics at the global and local level, Alberto Acosta explains:

> We, the ones that planned this, are questioning the system. We are talking about a post-extractivist economy, post-petroleum. We are looking for a different kind of organization of the society.
>
> I agree, it is [the Yasuní-ITT proposal] part of post-Kyoto but it does not fit into the logic of Kyoto. It is not like saying "Kyoto is over, we have to make a second Kyoto," like part two. But we are thinking it is from "Kyoto to Quito." That is our idea; make a leap. The ITT opens up a different vision. It is not the carbon market. It is not carbon bonds. It is not the traditional logic of mercantilizing the ecology. That is a clear matter to us.[62]

Esperanza Martínez, who is a vocal opponent of selling carbon bonds, or certificates, in voluntary carbon markets and/or the EU Emissions Trading Scheme, criticized the later versions of the Yasuní-ITT proposal for not being critical enough of Kyoto. In her discussions, she emphasized the original intention of the proposal as a criticism of Kyoto and a unique alternative. Martínez relates that

> The proposal was critical of Kyoto; however everything [in the current proposal] fits into Kyoto. Thus, it is a bit crazy . . . they [the CAD] do some negotiation in the sense of no emissions, so they can be a system comparable to Kyoto. And they launch a proposal of selling carbon bonds equivalent to Kyoto bonds. It has two problems: first, it is not recognized by the president, nor internationally, and second, it does not reinforce the original discourse critical of Kyoto. The most important part of the proposal, especially at the international level, was that they were presenting the common but differentiated responsibilities. On the contrary, there is a tacit renunciation because publicly it says, "come on, you have a great opportunity to keep on emitting carbon and we solve it," which was not the [original] idea.[63]

In her commentary, Martínez underlines the importance of "common but differentiated responsibilities." The Yasuní-ITT proposal picks up on the themes of such responsibilities from the 1992 Earth Summit, but goes even further. As Acosta et al. argue in a later analysis, the Yasuní-ITT proposal also must be a symbol to the world that Ecuador will do the ethically and morally correct thing: protect the ITT block, with or without global support, because it has a shared responsibility.[64] The concept of "shared responsibility" is significant because the authors also contend that placing blame on the industrialized world has only led to inaction; the Yasuní-ITT proposal is meant as a catalyst toward action with Ecuador in the lead.

Technical consultant Carlos Larrea agrees that the Kyoto Protocol is not sufficient for the developing world, particularly those fossil fuel–dependent. However, he argues that the Yasuní-ITT proposal does not need to be a reversal of Kyoto. In fact, he contends, "it is a third way . . . as Kyoto is something that is evolving. The intention of Kyoto is the fight against climate change . . . it is very rigid. That is why I think that the [Yasuní-ITT] mechanisms can be easily accepted as flexible mechanisms within Kyoto."[65]

Larrea conceptualizes the Kyoto Protocol not as something final, but rather as a work in progress. Thus, the insertion of parts of the Yasuní-ITT proposal in a future agreement on climate change is acceptable. He views this more as a global dialog seeking solutions, rather than a document against which to react. Unfortunately, the Copenhagen UNFCCC meeting in December 2009 did not result in an official statement of acceptance of the Yasuní-ITT proposal, nor did Ecuadorian government and UNDP officials sign the trust fund final agreement. However, Environment Minister Marcela Aguiñaga and Minister of Foreign Affairs Fander Falconí did present the proposal at the meeting, emphasizing Ecuador's commitment to it.

When asked if it were possible to change the Kyoto Protocol or create post-Kyoto standards, Yolanda Kakabadse answered:

> It is possible. We are involved because we believe in this. . . . For example yesterday I was in a forum and they were saying, "No, you cannot change Kyoto." We are not pretending to change Kyoto, first of all. Second of all, we are trying to make a post-Kyoto proposal with the support, at this moment, of Germany. And Germany says "if all the technical documents support the proposal and are solid enough, why don't we launch a pilot initiative?"[66]

Kakabadse further explained for critics of the Yasuní Guarantee Certificates (YGCs) that the proposal is meant to lead to a larger project:

> Perhaps an important reason why we believe that this is viable is not only because of the no-emissions issue, but because Kyoto has not benefited our countries. And I think there are many industrial countries (Annex 1) that view as troublesome the fact that the countries of the South are destroying our tropical forests, which have such a great potential; and we do not have instruments, a framework that allows us to be part of the solution. And here, it is not like we are selling our souls to the devil, as many think; but we are proposing to be part of the solution, global solutions in partnership.[67]

Kakabadse emphasizes an important underlying issue of this proposal: its southern origin. While presenters of the proposal argue that it revolutionizes environmental norms and couples them with human rights, beneath the surface they also argue for voices and new alternatives from poor countries with "the curse of abundance."[68] The challenge with this proposal will be to go beyond Ecuador's borders to other Amazonian and megadiverse countries for support, something that has not happened yet. Furthermore, aspects of the proposal in areas of deforestation include REDD mechanisms that have yet to be approved by the UNFCCC at the time of this writing. Thus, the Yasuní-ITT proposal encompasses various new struggles from the South regarding climate change and solutions from those countries, which, according to recent World Bank studies, will suffer the most as global temperatures rise.[69]

Human Rights and Uncontacted Peoples

In August 2009, the Human Rights Council Expert Mechanism on the Rights of Indigenous Peoples prepared guidelines for the protection of human rights of uncontacted peoples. These guidelines, in addition to International Labor Organization (ILO) convention 169, the Universal Declaration of Human Rights, and article 27 of the International Covenant on Civil and Political Rights, compose the framework for international legal mechanisms of such rights protection. The Expert Mechanism on the Rights of Indigenous Peoples is the new international body that covers indigenous issues and replaces the International Working Group on Indigenous Populations. The guidelines, based on international legal precedent, emphasize the absolute protection of indigenous peoples in voluntary isolation (uncontacted) and ask that member nations not infringe upon the territories of uncontacted peoples, nor try to contact them. They call for the self-determination of uncontacted peoples and for national and international laws that establish buffer zones for their continued existence within safe, autonomous territories. Moreover, these guidelines highlight the enmeshed existence of uncontacted indigenous peoples within their natural environments. Because of their dependence on their environment and vice versa, the guidelines call for the right to protect such environments. When a government becomes aware of such peoples within its borders, these guidelines call upon governments to protect the survival of these peoples over the economic gains of natural resource extraction. Finally, the Human Rights Council underlines the importance of these uncontacted peoples, not only in terms of their equal coverage of human rights, but as an important part of human cultural and ethnic diversity that should not be lost.[70]

It is within this normative context that the Yasuní-ITT proposal is placed. While Ecuador has conceded rights to uncontacted peoples, oil extraction in the ITT block would be a violation of such protections. As previously discussed, contacted and uncontacted indigenous peoples have voiced their concerns and their desire to remain in isolation. While international guidelines are part of the institutionalization of norms, they do not demonstrate the internalization of these norms within actors and as a basis for social movements. However, the words of those involved in the Yasuní-ITT campaign illustrate their keen awareness of the uncontacted indigenous peoples in Yasuní National Park and their desire to protect some of the world's last groups of peoples living in isolation.

While Peruvian president Alan García has publicly declared his doubts that uncontacted indigenous peoples exist in the Peruvian Amazon, Ecuador believes that they exist because uncontacted peoples have violently resisted incursions into their areas. As Pablo Fajardo, director of the Committee of Human Rights in Sucumbíos, Ecuador, explains:

> I think it is important to understand their languages. About a year or so ago, there were some bloody occurrences, homicides in the Waorani zone, and it was an interesting case. First, the Taromenane possibly spear a person, but with only one lance. But, before this, they gave signals—spears in trees where people had been, such as loggers or other people who had entered their territory. No one paid attention; they continued. Later, somebody was killed with a spear; and since it was only one person, they continued. Later, a few were killed with various spears in their bodies. Thus, their language must be understood. They do not speak verbally; or they do, but we do not understand their language. But this other kind of language, if they leave a spear, if they leave a signal, what does it mean? "Do not trespass," "Please do not trespass, it is dangerous." But you do not understand and continue. I think they put seven spears in someone. Imagine the time that it takes for a Taromenane to make a spear—it is a great sacrifice. They leave their message "this is a war." Their language has to be understood. They are saying, "World, do not trespass; leave us alone," but in their own language and it has to be understood.[71]

Fajardo agrees with the findings of the Human Rights Council. He contends that Ecuador is "extracting the wrong treasure" from the Amazon.[72] The Yasuní-ITT proposal, while focused on climate change initiatives, strongly supports the protection of the world's other treasure: our cultural and biological diversity.

Another aspect of the Yasuní-ITT dilemma is the knowledge of conflict surrounding the area. As Natalia Greene of Fundación Pachamama explains:

> In this whole issue about seismic testing that has been done, a lot of cases have been found—spears have been found and loggers have been killed. When you are an environmentalist, you don't care much about the life of loggers, but the

issue about the logger's or the oil man's right to live have to be included, and also the rights of the uncontacted indigenous people, because we are putting them in a situation of war. It is dangerous. There are and there will be killings.[73]

Thus, the ethical and moral dilemma runs far greater than merely extracting petroleum and damaging water supplies. It calls into question the survival of a group of human beings as a distinct community. Moreover, evidence of conflict and warnings for the future are difficult to ignore on local, national, and international levels.

CAD technical advisor, Carlos Larrea, illustrates aspects of social learning regarding the protection of uncontacted peoples. He cites the "deplorable living conditions" within which contacted Waorani communities live. These peoples were contacted in the 1980s and 1990s by the Summer Institute of Linguistics, a missionary organization, and oil access roads were built within their territories. However, their living standards have only continued to decline, as the majority live within the park and around various oil extraction sites.[74] Their traditional nomadic hunting has been left behind. Some have turned to illegal logging. Still others use shotguns given by oil companies to hunt. According to a recent scientific study by Wildlife Conservation Society and La Universidad San Francisco de Quito, such trends have led to overhunting of species—some of which are now endangered.[75]

Even those actors not involved in the Yasuní-ITT proposal, such as oil company representatives, agree that relating with the Waorani from a Western perspective is challenging. Repsol-YPF has the block that is closest to ITT and within Waorani territory. Its representative, Federico Cruz, admitted that working with the Waorani over their fifteen-year period in Block 16 "has not been easy." He said that you "learn as you go" and that "no one truly knows the Waorani because they are so recently contacted."[76] Cruz, while not opposed to working within Waorani communities, related the serious level of conflict in the *zona intangible*, which is near the border of their oil block.

The normative foundations of human rights that inform the Yasuní-ITT proposal include the rights of peoples in isolation to remain in their territories undisturbed and uncontacted. They underline the symbiotic relationship between uncontacted peoples and their environment, thus maintaining the importance of legal territories with the right to govern themselves. These norms have been officially accepted by Ecuador, having legalized a *zona intangible*. The Yasuní-ITT proposal is unique in that it recognizes the false boundaries between society and the environment, such as those between the Taromenane and the Tagaeri and Yasuní National Park; it intertwines the relationship between humans, their communities, and the environment in which they live. Thus, the Yasuní-ITT proposal makes global climate change not only an environmental imperative, but one of basic human survival.

Debates on Development and the Good Life

Perhaps one of the central and most challenging normative dialogs of the Yasuní-ITT plan is the concept of sustainable development and how to achieve "the good life." While those who originally developed and supported the Yasuní-ITT plan contend that the "good life" is achieved by post-materialist public policies that focus on societal well-being in areas of clean environment, health, and education, others who also support the plan argue that materialist foundations, such as the market, are unavoidable. The dichotomy among actors is not so stark, but the dialog surrounding the idea of leaving oil underground in the ITT block is indicative of larger fissures not just in Ecuador, but in other societies around the globe, about how to live sustainably.

Sumak kawsay, the good life, is the integrating theme of the new Ecuadorian constitution of 2008. It signifies a turn away from a society and an economy based solely on market and profit-driven growth toward a new form of democratic development. It encompasses social, economic, and environmental guarantees and rights for people and for nature.[77] The good life is not a prescription, nor is the process that defines it. Rather, it is social and natural construction that changes as society deems necessary and nature warrants.[78]

One of the most strident criticisms within the concept of *sumak kawsay* is that of economies established on markets driven by profit only. This concept obligates state leaders to consider society's and nature's well-being over earnings, which, according to Edgardo Lander, has the potential to create a richer society and democracy; but rich in terms of quality of life for all.[79] In this sense, Eduardo Gudynas, consultant to the Constituent Assembly for the 2008 constitution, argues that approaching the good life may mean leaving behind material objects. For example, he says that the coat we buy should be practical and protect us from the rain, rather than reflecting a brand name purely for "ostentatious" reasons.[80] The idea is to grow an economy based on society, not profits, and to value wealth in terms of the quantity of people who are housed, clothed, nourished, and educated, rather than the quantity of imports and exports.

The Yasuní-ITT Initiative in many ways is indicative of the struggle to define the good life, both in Ecuador and globally. It emphasizes people over petroleum and human rights over company rights. However, the role of the market in finding our way to the good life has been challenging and continues to be debated. Some actors, including Gudynas, Acosta, Martínez, and Acción Ecológica and their colleagues in the campaign Amazonía por la Vida (Amazon for Life), contend that market strategies only exacerbate the problem by giving polluters a buyout to continue destroying nature. On the other hand, actors just as dedicated to the initiative, including CAD members Yolanda Kakabadse,

Francisco Carrión, Roque Sevilla, and technical advisor Carlos Larrea argue that a combination of donations and market strategies is the most prudent and still achieves the goal of protecting the ITT block. Thus, one of the biggest unresolved issues of contention within the proposal is selling Yasuní Guarantee Certificates (YGCs) in carbon markets, effectively selling avoided emissions to those who need to meet emissions limits or pay if they overpollute.

Pablo Fajardo of the Human Rights Committee in Sucumbíos argues that "it is a concept that makes me think because it is like someone who has the money saying,'Ok, I am going to pay 1,000 or 5,000 dollars to keep on contaminating.' Those kinds of things are contradictory."[81] Yet, realistically, Federico Starnfeld of the German International Cooperation Enterprise (GIZ) admits, "I have a very strange disjuncture right now because I say, 'well, which was the proposal that Acción Ecológica made at the beginning? Preserve that; receive 350 million dollars for goodwill?' But that did not make any sense. Now it is transformed to something that can sell eco-systemic services."[82]

Former secretary of the initiative, Juana Ramos, concludes that

> We all would like to have completely generous economies in which everybody would think about the common well-being, but it is not real. We can find one, two, five people who would be willing to do something completely altruistic, but it does not correspond to reality. Because if that was the general tonic we would not have poverty in the world; it is a reality.[83]

However, Eduardo Gudynas rejects the notion that the good life is too altruistic to achieve. Regarding Yasuní-ITT he argues that Ecuador cannot ask for compensation without recognizing its own responsibility in the environmental degradation of the Amazon.[84] International compensation for leaving oil underground assumes that there is a party that owes Ecuador for the destruction and that the Ecuadorian state should be compensated. However, the Ecuadorian state is simultaneously the guilty party for giving out oil contracts that pollute and the benefactor of funds to keep oil underground. Furthermore, the Ecuadorian state cannot obligate compensation for something that it is already obligated to do according to its constitution.[85] Gudynas's solution is to make the Yasuní-ITT plan a public policy, rather than a market solution. Success is based on political negotiation and dialog, rather than on the amount of money compensated or not. This level of responsibility and policy making can range from local to international levels.

When asked what the alternative public policy would be, Esperanza Martínez answered that their original proposal was "perfect." She explained:

> We used to say: do not extract the crude oil. A mechanism of compensations can be created, compensations in cash or linked to a modality that works against the

schemes of the petroleum transition, of post-petroleum Ecuador. If there are energy investments they should be in alternative sources of energy, accomplishing the objective of the post-petroleum society. And our proposal was fresh funds with symbolic crude sales, paid by the citizens: "I want to buy a barrel." "My mom was saying she was going to buy twenty." It was an ideal model. We would not sell anything. We would not yield on sovereignty. We were going to be critical of Kyoto. It was an example for the global citizenship to mobilize against climate change; it was perfect.[86]

While actors that straddle both sides of this divide disagree on how to achieve the protection of Yasuní, they all agree on keeping the oil underground and the need for a post-petroleum economy. The process of alternative norm creation in this facet of the proposal is nascent and not yet internalized by all actors. While the Ecuadorian state is proposing the sale of YGCs in voluntary markets and possibilities in a post-Kyoto EU ETS, its civil society supporters are subtly criticizing this method of payment.

This debate in many ways is symbolic of larger international debates on the issue of how to protect the environment and what goals we would like to achieve as a world community. Many of the Copenhagen 2009 and Cancun 2010 UNFCCC talks have revolved around alternative proposals, such as REDD, from developing countries. At the same time, the United States is debating a cap-and-trade system that would enlarge its carbon market trading. The question that some are asking is whether solutions based on profit, not people and nature, obfuscate the realities and only engender further pollution. The Yasuní-ITT proposal pushes the normative struggles of man, nature, and market to the limit by calling for a global dialog about how the planet can survive if all countries follow the capitalist, market-based path of industrialization motored by fossil fuels without a plan to conserve and protect the planet.

Notes

1. Rafael Correa, "Yasuní-ITT," May 30, 2009, http://www.youtube.com/user/YasuniITT#p/a/f/0/_dg48IM9gwM (accessed December 20, 2009).

2. Esperanza Martínez, interview, Quito, Ecuador, January 20, 2009.

3. Ibid. Translation by author.

4. Alberto Acosta, "El Buen Vivir, una oportunidad por construir," *Portal de Economía Solidaria*, February 17, 2009.

5. Alberto Acosta, interview, Quito, Ecuador, February 27, 2009. Translation by author.

6. Ibid.

7. Ibid. Translation by author.

8. Interview with multinational oil company representative, Quito, Ecuador, 2009. Translation by author.

9. "El Buen Vivir, un concepto cuyas metas se proyectan a largo plazo," *El Universo*, October 19, 2009.

10. Carlos Larrea, interview, Quito, Ecuador, January 23, 2009.

11. Fander Falconí and Carlos Larrea, "Impactos ambientales de las políticas de liberalización externa y los flujos de capital: el caso de Ecuador," in *Globalización y Desarrollo en América Latina*, ed. Fander Falconí, Marcelo Hercowitz, and Roldan Muradian (Quito, Ecuador: FLACSO, 2004).

12. *The Stern Review on the Economics of Climate Change* is the largest (700 pages) and most widely known report which discusses the effect of global warming on the world economy. It was released on October 30, 2006, by economist Nicholas Stern for the British government.

13. Carlos Larrea, interview, Quito, Ecuador, January 23, 2009.

14. Ibid. Translation by author.

15. Carl Ross, e-mail message to author, December 10, 2010.

16. "Canje de Deuda a cambio de no explotar el petróleo del Yasuní," *Diario La Hora*, May 24, 2007.

17. Martínez, interview, Quito, Ecuador, January 20, 2009. Translation by author.

18. Federico Starnfeld's interview materials reflect his personal opinions and not those of the GIZ. Any analysis of the role of the GTZ is based on the author's examination of the data.

19. Federico Starnfeld, interview, Quito, Ecuador, February 10, 2009. Translation by author.

20. Larrea, interview, Quito, Ecuador, January 23, 2009. Translation by author.

21. Acosta, interview, Quito, Ecuador, February 27, 2009. Translation by author.

22. Roque Sevilla, telephone interview, Quito, Ecuador, February 6, 2009. Translation by author.

23. Yolanda Kakabadse, interviews, Quito, Ecuador, January 21 and April 13, 2009. Translation by author.

24. Francisco Carrión, interview, Quito, Ecuador, March 26, 2009. Translation by author.

25. Ibid. Translation by author.

26. Ibid. Translation by author.

27. "Francisco Carrión, 'Mi reto será concretar el proyecto del ITT del Ecuador,'" *El Universo*, October 19, 2009.

28. Jeffrey Checkel, "Why Comply? Social Learning and European Identity Change," *International Organization* 55, no. 3 (Summer 2001).

29. Allison Brysk, *From Tribal Village to Global Village: Indian Rights and International Relations in Latin America* (Stanford, CA: Stanford University Press, 2000); Pamela Martin, *The Globalization of Contentious Politics: The Amazonian Indigenous Rights Movement* (New York: Routledge, 2003); Pamela Martin and Franke Wilmer, "Transnational Normative Struggles and Globalization: The Case of Indigenous Peoples in Bolivia and Ecuador," *Globalizations* 5, no. 4 (December 2008).

30. Starnfeld, interview, Quito, Ecuador, February 10, 2009. Translation by author.

31. Ibid. Translation by author.

32. Ecuador Yasuní-ITT Trust Fund: Terms of Reference, July 28, 2010, United Nations Development Programme Multidonor Trust Fund Office, http://mdtf.undp.org/yasuni. Per a telephone conversation with UN ambassador Francisco Carrión in August 2010, the terms of reference are guidelines. Funding mechanisms may need to be flexible according to contributor and Ecuadorian government negotiations; Starnfeld, e-mail communication to author, December 15, 2010.

33. José Vicente Troya, interview, Quito, Ecuador, February 18, 2009. Translation by author.

34. Ibid. Translation by author.

35. It is important to note Sevilla's interest in meshing the proposal with market-based economic strategies.

36. Pablo Fajardo, interview, Quito, Ecuador, February 6, 2009. Translation by author.

37. Kevin Koenig, interview, Quito, Ecuador, April 13, 2009.

38. Ibid.

39. From Pachamama Alliance's website, http://www.pachamama.org/content/view/2/4/.

40. Natalia Greene, interview, Quito, Ecuador, February 12, 2009. Translation by author.

41. Originally, this study was conducted to demonstrate the devastating effects of roads in the Amazon for possible drilling in Block 31, which is next to the ITT block. It was later revised to include the effort to protect the ITT block.

42. "Scientists Concerned for Yasuní," November 25, 2004.

43. Matt Finer, e-mail message to author, November 25, 2009.

44. Margot S. Bass, Matt Finer, Clinton N. Jenkins, Holger Kreft, Diego F. Cisneros-Heredia, et al. "Global Conservation Significance of Ecuador's Yasuní National Park," *PLoS ONE* 5, no. 1: e8767. doi:10.1371/journal.pone.0008767.

45. Verónica Quitigüiña, interview, Quito, Ecuador, March 4, 2009. Translation by author.

46. Matt Finer et al., "Ecuador's Yasuní Biosphere Reserve: A Brief Modern History and Conservation Challenges," *IOP Publishing Environmental Research*, July–September 2009, doi:10.1088/1748-9326/4/3/034005; Matt Finer et al., "Oil and Gas Projects in the Western Amazon: Threats to Wilderness, Biodiversity, and Indigenous Peoples," *PLoS ONE* 3, no. 8 (2008): e2932. doi:10.1371/journal.pone.0002932.

47. Matt Finer, "Ecuador Seeks Compensation to Leave Amazon Oil Undisturbed," *Environment News Service* (April 24, 2007).

48. Finer et al., "Ecuador's Yasuní Biosphere Reserve."

49. Peter Haas, "Do Regimes Matter? Epistemic Communities and Mediterranean Pollution Control," *International Organization* 43, no. 3 (Summer 1989): 377–403.

50. Pablo Flores, interview, Quito, Ecuador, March 25, 2009. Translation by author.

51. Ibid. Translation by author.

52. Ibid. Translation by author.

53. Ibid. Translation by author.

54. Federico Cruz, interview, Quito, Ecuador, March 20, 2009. Translation by author.

55. Ibid.; Rene Ortiz, interview, Quito, Ecuador, March 23, 2009. Translations by author.

56. Cruz, interview, Quito, Ecuador, March 20, 2009. Translation by author.

57. The final point was communicated by Dr. Matt Finer, Save America's Forests, November 25, 2009. Yet Sven Wunder, *Oil Wealth and the Fate of the Forest: A Comparative Study of Eight Tropical Countries* (New York: Routledge, 2003), argues that deforestation was lower in some cases of oil development (not in Ecuador).

58. Ortiz, interview, Quito, Ecuador, March 23, 2009. Translation by author.

59. Ibid.

60. Cruz, interview, Quito, Ecuador, March 20, 2009. Translation by author.

61. Alberto Acosta, *La Maldición de la Abundancia* (Quito, Ecuador: Abya Yala, 2009).

62. Acosta, interview, Quito, Ecuador, February 27, 2009. Translation by author.

63. Martínez, interview, Quito, Ecuador, January 20, 2009. Translation by author. At the time of this interview, President Correa had not officially approved the Yasuní-ITT proposal funding mechanisms.

64. Acosta et al., "A Political, Economic, and Ecological Initiative in the Ecuadorian Amazon," Americas Program Policy Report, http://americas.irc-online.org/am/6345 (accessed July 30, 2010).

65. Larrea, interview, Quito, Ecuador, January 23, 2009. Translation by author.

66. Kakabadse, interviews, Quito, Ecuador, January 21, and April 13, 2009. Translations by author.

67. Ibid. Translation by author.

68. Acosta, "El Buen Vivir."

69. Michael von Bülow, "World Bank: Poor Countries Will Be Hit Hardest," United Nations Climate Change Conference, December 7–18, 2009 (November 5, 2009), http://en.cop15.dk/news/view+news?newsid=2272.

70. "Expert Mechanism on the Rights of Indigenous Peoples," Human Rights Council, June 30, 2009, http://www2.ohchr.org/english/issues/indigenous/ExpertMechanism/2nd/docs/A_HRC_EMRIP_2009_6.pdf.

71. Fajardo, interview, Quito, Ecuador, February 6, 2009. Translation by author.

72. Ibid. Translation by author.

73. Greene, interview, Quito, Ecuador, February 12, 2009. Translation by author.

74. Larrea, interview, Quito, Ecuador, January 23, 2009. Translation by author.

75. Julie Larsen Maher, "Oil and Wildlife Don't Mix in Ecuador's Eden," Wildlife Conservation Society/Physorg.com, September 10, 2009.

76. Cruz, interview, Quito, Ecuador, March 20, 2009. Translation by author.

77. Alberto Acosta and Esperanza Martínez, *El Buen Vivir: Una vía para el desarrollo* (Quito, Ecuador: Abya Yala, 2009), 7.

78. Acosta, "El Buen Vivir," 19.

79. Edgardo Lander, "Hacía otra noción de riqueza," in *El Buen Vivir: Una vía para el desarrollo,*" ed. Alberto Acosta and Esperanza Martínez (Quito, Ecuador: Abya Yala, 2009).

80. Eduardo Gudynas, "Seis puntos clave en ambiente y desarrollo," in *El Buen Vivir: Una vía para el desarrollo*, ed. Alberto Acosta and Esperanza Martínez (Quito, Ecuador: Abya Yala, 2009), 128.

81. Fajardo, interview, Quito, Ecuador, February 6, 2009. Translation by author.

82. Starnfeld, interview, Quito, Ecuador, February 10, 2009. Translation by author.

83. Juana Ramos, interview, Quito, Ecuador, March 6, 2009. Translation by author.

84. Eduardo Gudynas, *El Mandato Ecológico: Derechos de la naturaleza y políticas ambientales en la nueva Constitución* (Quito, Ecuador: Abya Yala, 2009).

85. Ibid., 138–141.

86. Martínez, interview, Quito, Ecuador, January 20, 2009. Translation by author.

6

The Future of Global Governance in the Amazon

The Yasuní Effect

WHILE THE YASUNÍ-ITT PROPOSAL presents a novel approach to climate change at a time when some scientists are arguing that the planet has passed a threshold, or tipping point, the Amazonian region still faces a great many challenges. Major natural gas reserves have been discovered by Petrobras in the Peruvian Amazon, and Peru has accelerated its pace of oil block concessions. On the Ecuadorian border, Colombia is also looking to capitalize on newly discovered reserves. Additionally, drug trafficking between the two countries is still a significant security threat to the peoples that live in the region. Due to these threats and unresolved issues on their border, diplomatic relations between the countries have cooled. Local peoples tell stories of drug smugglers and increased drug use in the region, which they say have also led to dangerous living conditions for them and their families. Many people who work in the region warned during interviews that travel to the Colombian border was not safe. This insecurity is combined with another environmental hazard: glyphosate spraying of coca plantations near the Ecuadorian border. The Ecuadorian government is pursuing a halt to this activity through the Organization of American States and the Inter-American Commission on Human Rights (IAHCR). Together with massive deforestation and illegal logging, these environmental issues tell the tale of paradise on the brink of being lost forever.

The preceding chapters outline a glimmer of hope for those in the region and others around the world who strive toward a more sustainable living plan. While it is obvious that climate change challenges affect the entire planet, the solutions to global governance have been lacking. The Kyoto Pro-

PHOTO 6.1
The Tiputini River, near Yasuní National Park.
Source: Bill Martin.

tocol was never ratified by the one of the world's major polluters, the United States. China—having the highest carbon emissions on the planet—and developing countries that are the most affected by climate change are not among the Annex 1 countries included in the treaty for which caps would be binding. International organizations (like the IPCC, the UNFCCC, and the UNEP) exist to deal with the issue, but their enforcement capability is limited. Commonly ratified global policies did not emerge from these bodies. Some call for a World Environment Organization (WEO), but in the meantime, the Yasuní-ITT Initiative has enthusiastic supporters who believe that there is no precedent for their proposal and no roadmap to follow.

Given the relatively recent nature of the proposal and the massive amount of civil and political organization and mobilization it has taken over a multi-year period, this book seeks to account for the steps along the way toward a post-petroleum and post-Kyoto future. The analysis of the global and local dimensions required to assemble an innovative design from such an unlikely candidate (an oil-dependent poor country) is meant to provide guideposts for those in the policy world and/or state leaders seeking to replicate such an activity. It is also meant to inspire others who have experienced the sickening effects of oil pollution in their own towns. No one told the CAD and other civil society members that this project would be easy, nor did they start their journey with the plan in place. It was crafted after much local, national, and international dialog, debate, and policy development. The moral of the story is "Never say never."

From the perspective of those of us who study the complex web of global governance, this case illustrates the changes in the international system since the globalization of politics and economics throughout the 1990s. While the Ecuadorian state and its charismatic leader Rafael Correa are officially presenting this plan to other world leaders and organizations, international civil society is also mobilized to support it, and at the same time, keep a critical distance from it. As Paul J. Nelson and Ellen Dorsey conclude, "the violating state" is no longer an accurate representation of world politics.[1] Rather, they contend the global acceptance and formation of international laws and treaties regarding human rights have changed NGO strategies toward a more rights-based approach.[2] The social environmental justice movement embraces the strategizing of these rights, while also seeking to push environmental concerns to the forefront on the world stage.

Dorsey and Nelson examine new rights advocacy from the perspective of NGOs and their changing strategies based on accepted international rights.[3] Risse-Kappen and Keck and Sikkink analyze advocacy networks from the perspective of states and NGOs with norms guiding the processes.[4] This analysis incorporates their contributions to thought on transnational networks and adds the element of the individual actors and social learning to their palate. As demonstrated in the preceding chapters, the Yasuní-ITT campaign exists because critical political actors and civil society leaders challenged accepted international norms on climate change (the Kyoto Protocol) and economic and political structures based on natural resource extraction to present an alternative plan to and for the planet.

The path to alternative norm creation included domestic and international processes. At the domestic level, Ecuador has adopted a new constitution that gives nature rights and seeks the good life for its citizens, emphasizing the right to live in harmony with nature. The constitutional process consisted of a constituent assembly that was democratically voted into power, as well as civil society organizations that supported the process and gave feedback. The constitution was accepted by Ecuadorians in September 2008 in a democratic referendum vote. According to this document, natural resource extraction is prohibited in national parks and indigenous peoples living in isolation have the right to continue to do so. Thus, the Yasuní-ITT proposal incorporates norms from Ecuadorian society.

At the global level, the proposal intertwines human rights for uncontacted indigenous peoples, following the IAHCR ruling of precautionary measures in 2006 and Human Rights Council guidelines for indigenous peoples living in voluntary isolation—an example of rights advocacy as viewed by Nelson and Dorsey.[5] Furthermore, it advances global norms on climate change in four areas: 1) solutions from the developing world—particularly those from fossil fuel–dependent, megadiverse countries; 2) a shift in thinking from carbon sequestration and limits to avoided emissions; 3) the social consequences of climate change; and 4) a replicable plan to protect biodiversity in one of the most biodiverse places on the planet. On another, more controversial level, the Yasuní-ITT proposal represents alternative economic solutions for post-petroleum societies. The controversy of this element is whether carbon trading and markets should be a part of the proposal.

To this end, the CAD and some members of civil society disagree. CAD president Roque Sevilla (July 2008–January 2010) defends market solutions to trade avoided emissions through CGYs as a practical approach to selling Ecuador's environment as a service to the planet, rather than its oil. Juana Ramos, his predecessor in the initiative, agrees. However, Acción Ecológica and its *minga* collaborators (allied organizations who act in coordination with Acción), Amazon Watch, Save America's Forests, and World Resources Institute, have their doubts. Their opinions range from concerns that carbon markets provide a free ticket to polluters to objections to markets as the solution, preferring conservation and radical changes in the industrial-consumer complex. This debate highlights the unspoken tension among supporters of the plan. While all agree that saving ITT and protecting the uncontacted groups is the ultimate goal, the method of funding for them is linked to normative foundations on the good life, international politics, and the future of climate change treaties.

Such tension underscores the bargaining process to form new, alternative norms and institutionalize them. As of this writing, the minister of natural and cultural heritage has signed various funding agreements for the trust fund. The first country to commit funds was China with a $1 million contribution and a $20,000 contribution from the members of its Ecuadorian embassy. Chile has committed $100,000. Spain has committed $1.3 million dollars and the possibility of a multi-year commitment for other funds. Italy is in negotiations with the Ecuadorian government to contribute funds via debt cancellation of $38 million of its $58 million debt with the country. One innovative feature of the Yasuní Trust Fund is the ability of any person or organization to contribute funds. During the Cancun Climate Change talks of the UNFCCC in December 2010, the regional government of Wallonia in Belgium was the first European regional government to contribute, donating $398,000 to the trust fund.[6] Germany, previously its major contributor, has stated that it may not contribute to the Yasuní-ITT Trust Fund, citing inconsistencies in the guarantees of the Trust Fund.[7] The Ecuadorian government has responded to these concerns and is awaiting a formal response. Meanwhile, Ecuador is pursuing the Yasuní-ITT Initiative vigorously, as evidenced by the high-level team at the Cancun Climate Change meetings in December 2010 that included President Correa, Foreign Minister Ricardo Patiño, Minister of Natural and Cultural Heritage María Fernanda Espinosa, and Environmental Minister Marcela Aguiñaga.[8]

Ironing Out the Details

While the proposal presented in chapter 4 was relatively detailed, some governmental and financial structures of the plan are still vague. As CAD officials jet around the globe enticing the world to invest in avoided carbon emissions and their "big idea from a small country," many Waorani leaders and local government officials are wondering what the plan actually is and how it pertains to them. When asked if the CAD had worked with the Waorani leadership, their answer was "not very much."[9] Juana Ramos and Yolanda Kakabadse cited meetings with local people and indigenous leaders about the initiative, but in an information session format only. Each expressed their desire to have more contact in the local ITT area, but also had their reservations. Yolanda Kakabadse spoke of a meeting that she had in Coca to explain the CAD plan with local Waorani leaders and mayor Anita Rivas. However, she said that she did not want to work too closely with local populations until funding for the proposal was guaranteed. There are two problems with this political strategy: 1) Elinor Ostrom,[10] Robert Putnam,[11] and others have found that community governance involvement signals effective policy outcomes; and 2) the Waorani may be the best people to market the initiative and to direct development dollars in their area. A number of NGO representatives (among them Amazon Watch and Save America's Forests) commented that they were disappointed in the lack of communication and collaboration between the CAD and local Amazonian peoples. To remedy this disconnect, Save America's Forests is working with the CAD to "promote better dialog between the Waorani and the ITT Team."[12]

As of September 2009, efforts at communication with local peoples in the Yasuní National Park area had not been successful. According to a survey of residents in the Francisco de Orellana province, where the park is located, only 27.93 percent of those living in the park's region knew that it was a national park. While 85.91 percent of those surveyed from twelve cantons within the province claimed that they were interested in supporting conservation measures for the park, only 11 percent were aware of the Yasuní-ITT Initiative and proposal. Yet, when local peoples were asked if they would be interested in preserving the park and maintaining it for reasons of biodiversity and natural resources, over 92 percent responded favorably. Thus, local support for the goals of the proposal exists. The challenge for the latest members of the CAD will be to communicate the details of the plan with local citizens and engage them in the initiative.[13]

The crux of the Yasuní-ITT proposal is leaving oil underground to lead the Earth down a post-petroleum road toward the good life. The revolutionary concept was avoiding emissions. However, in late October 2009, according to *El Universo* newspaper, president Rafael Correa met with his Russian counterpart, Dimitri Medvedev, during which time both countries signed an agreement of cooperation to allow Russian companies OAO Zarubezhneft and OAO Sroy Transgaz with Petroecuador "to explore and exploit Block 31," the adjoining block to ITT, also within Yasuní National Park and the Waorani Ethnic Reserve.[14] When CAD officials were asked their thoughts on this issue and its impacts on the Yasuní-ITT Initiative, they too were confounded. This issue is significant because it not only questions Ecuador's resolve and commitment to protecting the park and uncontacted indigenous peoples, it also flouts the post-petroleum, path-breaking approach toward climate change that President Correa and his country allegedly support. Some members of civil society have been so outraged by such a tactic by President Correa that they have suggested that contributing countries tie their funding to not only leaving oil underground in ITT, but leaving it in Block 31 in particular.[15] Lastly, the policy disjuncture between the CAD and the president, and presumably the Ministry of Energy and Mines, brings into question the level of authority and institutionalization of the CAD within the government.

As President Correa announced in March 2010 the process of applying for licensure for drilling in the ITT block, another red flag was raised regarding the government's commitment to the Yasuní-ITT proposal. While President Correa assures citizens that this is simply part of his original Plan B—to drill if funding is not acquired—others argue that such tactics undermine the vitality and international capacity necessary to capture such funding. Furthermore, current CAD president Ivonne Baki sought funding from Iran for the initiative, a country with which Ecuador shared a spot on the list of countries that the Financial Action Task Force (FATF) in February 2010 designated as having deficiencies in its financial regulations regarding money laundering.[16] Such associations could hurt the proposal and its future funding.

Global funding for developing countries and climate change is picking up. Ecuador, however, has lost some of these opportunities, given its rejection of the World Bank. For example, the World Bank, in conjunction with other multilateral banks, has established the Clean Technology Fund, a $40 million fund that supports technology and programming for lower carbon emissions. Additionally, there is the South-South Trust Fund through the World Bank in which developing countries share technology and ideas on sustainable development initiatives from the South. Finally, World Bank Climate Investment Funds have totaled over $6.14 billion in donations from the industrialized world to support climate programs, most specifically in the area of pilot projects from the developing world. Such a rejection of the global status quo institutions may hinder the ultimate ability of the CAD to not only fund the initiative, but also to embed it into a broader global governance framework for replication.

Finally, in April 2010, the United States announced that those countries opposed to the Copenhagen Accord from December 2009 may lose US funds for climate change initiatives in the developing world. Ecuador stands to lose $2.5 million due to its opposition to the Copenhagen Accord.[17] While CAD president Ivonne Baki announced that she was working with the US on this position and the US agreed that this ruling is not yet determined, Ecuador's contrary stance could threaten its ultimate collection of funds for the project. Such discord with global governance institutions and mechanisms illustrates the challenges in proposing new norms within existing frameworks of global governance.

The expansion of the initiative to the entire park was always a goal of civil society members. The possible concession of Block 31 to the Russian government and lost World Bank funding opportunities are certainly setbacks in this area. Additionally, funding for the initiative will be directed not just to Yasuní National Park, but throughout the country as a means of implementing the National Development Plan. As seen in chapter 3, the park is severely underfunded and Amazonian provinces suffer from poverty disproportionate to their Highland and Coastal neighbors. This emphasis on national development makes the Yasuní-ITT proposal significant to all Ecuadorians as theoretically they would have benefited from sales of petroleum in the block (although Acosta, Falconí and Larrea disagree with this argument).[18] However, it diminishes the previous version's emphasis on biodiversity and the protection of uncontacted peoples. If the plan is successful, such funding for national goals—the protection of Amazonian biodiversity and the rights of uncontacted peoples—would set an international precedent and create a replicable model for other megadiverse countries to follow.[19]

In November 2009, CAD member and Ecuadorian ambassador to the United Nations, Francisco Carrión, met with UN Secretary General Ban Ki-Moon and reviewed the Yasuní-ITT proposal. Carrión cited the secretary general's interest and support of the proposal, as well as his own work with the UNDP to finalize the international trust fund for the initiative.[20] At the time of this writing, CAD officials report that they are developing the national legal framework to support the international trust fund, but expect the details to be finalized soon. A key element in this UNDP guaranteed trust fund is the direct funding to projects throughout the country as listed in the National Development Plan. Supporters argue that such funding is insurance for the global community that Ecuador is serious about using these contributions to support its intended projects directly with international collaboration. Furthermore, the innovative financial and governance mechanisms created between Ecuador and the UNDP have the potential to set a new standard for states to achieve climate change goals without an international climate treaty supporting them.

The final details of the proposal that still remain unclear are the monitoring and project assessment mechanisms. The plan calls for a citizen oversight body and a citizen representative on the International Trust Fund Board, as well as direct interaction with Amazonian indigenous leaders. However, the plan does not outline the method of selection to such organizations—appointment or election. The plan also does not include non-voting experts in the fields of biodiversity or environmental management on the trust fund board or in the citizen oversight body. Furthermore, the plan does not explain the level of authority of these organizations or the method of resolution if their decisions differ from those of national government representatives. A clear delineation of political and governmental authority at all levels from local to global is lacking. If successful global governance mechanisms are to be implemented, such a flow chart of sorts for leaders, activists, and global citizens will be necessary for effective implementation and evaluation.

Along these lines, who will determine which national development programs are selected and who will rate their level of economic value? One of the main tenets of this proposal is that the one-time investment in the capital fund will generate enough income to create a revenue fund for these programs. Such promises are inspiring, but not real unless validated. Will there also be an assessment committee composed of local, national, and global authorities to evaluate initial project investment, completion, and generation of other environmental services, such as REDD-related projects? The Yasuní-ITT plan will only ultimately be successful and replicable if such evaluation is conducted in a timely manner and disseminated to the world community.

A final note of consideration is to new players in eventual post-Kyoto agreements. For example, the United States is considering climate change legislation and a possible cap-and-trade system. Such a system would implement market solutions to climate problems, including carbon markets. The CAD met with the Chicago Climate Exchange in November 2009 and is hopeful that new carbon market opportunities to trade CGYs might exist in the United States. Furthermore, China is seeking to develop climate change legislation. Ecuador is considering a $1 billion loan from China in the form of pre-payment for energy. If pre-payment of energy means petroleum, this may be a signal of increased extractive operations in the Amazon, possibly even in Block 31 or toward the southern Amazon. Alternatively, might China also participate in the purchase of CGYs in some future climate change agreement? The latter is clearly the better choice toward "the good life" and the implementation of the Yasuní-ITT proposal. Ideally, the Ecuadorians seek global acceptance of their plan through international treaty inclusion. However, they have been working on bilateral agreements until such inclusion presents itself.

Above and Below the Canopy:
Global Governance, Yasuní, and Climate Change Policy

The state is the sole owner of natural resources below the ground in Ecuador. Since 2006, the country has steadily increased the percentage of interest it shares with foreign oil companies. Such steps toward more state control over national resources include a 2010 renegotiation of all petroleum contracts so that companies are paid a flat fee for oil production, rather than the traditional profit sharing.[21] However, the case of leaving natural resources underground in exchange for avoided carbon emissions and shared responsibility for environmental degradation opens the ITT block of Yasuní National Park to the world community.

From the beginning of the initiative, the campaign to save ITT included international, local, and national actors. Carl Ross and Matt Finer tell the story of Alberto Acosta announcing the plan to them in May 2007 at the World Wildlife Fund (WWF) office in Washington, D.C., while they had a visiting Waorani leader present. The local-global nexus began with the minister of energy and mines announcing the initiative to a group of INGO representatives with a Waorani leader in the United States (Washington, D.C.) via videoconference; all this took place prior to the Ecuadorian government's official announcement from President Correa in Quito, in June 2007.[22] From May 2007 forward, the campaign ebbed and flowed with international and national interactions, debates, exchanges, and bargaining.

As demonstrated in the previous chapters, Acción Ecológica, Amazon Watch, Finding Species, GIZ, Pachamama and Fundación Pachamama,

PHOTO 6.2
Save America's Forests brought the Waorani to the Washington, D.C., press
conference at which Ecuador's ITT proposal was announced so they could participate.
With his back to the camera is Fernando Nihua, vice president of the Waorani
organization NAWE. Moi Enomenga is wearing the feathered crown. Manuela is
presidenta of AMWAE, the Waorani women's organization.
Source: Carl Ross, courtesy of Save America's Forests.

Save America's Forests, World Resources Institute, and the consulting bodies Climate Focus and Silvestrum, among other actors, played crucial roles in the following:

a) Getting the Yasuní-ITT proposal on international agendas—the Clinton Global Initiative, for example;
b) Providing significant scientific data and information about biodiversity and indigenous peoples—recent studies from Save America's Forests and the letter from the fifty-nine Scientists Concerned for Yasuní;
c) Connecting the Ministry of Foreign Affairs and the CAD members with local communities—information sessions in Coca;
d) Providing information on opportunities in the international community and/or limitations—the March 2009 CAD workshop and consultant input on carbon trading mechanisms and difficulties of entrance in the EU ETS;

e) Constructing the mechanisms within the plan—the debates over funding and trust fund; and
f) Connecting these organizations with leaders around the globe—the crucial role of GIZ and the German government.

These organizations have complex webs of social interactions. Some members, like Kevin Koenig of Amazon Watch, had interned with Acción Ecológica in previous years, and thus have strong personal ties with actors on the ground. Those that are located in Washington, D.C., often interact with one another, such as WRI and Save America's Forests, and collaborate on research findings about the park and the proposal. In this sense, Checkel's concept of social learning is crucial.[23] These actors have all participated in previous campaigns in Ecuador to some extent and have learned from the experiences, as well as from each other. The CAD seeks their support and consults with them regularly, as well as uses their scientific data and political leverage.

In the development of the proposal and the global governance mechanisms for the trust fund, the Ecuadorian state is working in conjunction with the UNDP to construct nationally and internationally acceptable institutions. Given the reliance on the UNDP, the state is not the sole purveyor of law. As the initiative outlines, the state will be the sovereign authority for program implementation, but the funds, according to Carlos Larrea and trust fund documents, will be directly given to projects and organizations, not the central bank. Thus, once natural resources are exchanged for planetary good in the form of avoided carbon emissions, global governance includes the state, but is not directed by it.

The global governance processes of this initiative began with norms that challenged those already established in the international system. Those norms that were challenged include a) Washington consensus neoliberal economics in favor of socialism of the twenty-first century; b) natural resource extraction in favor of post-petroleum policies; and c) sustainable development based on modernization, industrialization, and markets in favor of politics of the good life. The international norms that were included in the initiative were those of human rights and indigenous rights through the IAHCR and those from the socio-environmental movement that links environmental degradation and poverty. The challenged norms arose out of massive citizen mobilization that began in Ecuador in the 1990s with the indigenous rights movement and the environmental movement. The culmination on a national level of the quest for these rights was the passage of the 2008 constitution, which gave rights to nature and indigenous peoples—contacted and uncontacted—and based the economy and public policy on the search for the good life, or humans living in harmony with nature through constant democratic dialog.

As discussed in chapter 4, Ecuador has defaulted on its Global Bonds and bought them back for 30 percent of their value. It has renegotiated contracts with Perenco, Agip, and Repsol-YPF, and awaits arbitration hearings with Occidental Oil Company—which it ousted from the country in May 2006. In November and December 2010, it renegotiated contracts with private oil companies toward a contract of services, rather than profit-sharing for petroleum extraction. The country has also removed the IMF and World Bank representatives and is working toward a Banco del Sur with its other South American neighbors. In this respect, it has challenged the previously accepted Washington consensus policies. However, Ecuador is also looking to expand its natural resource extraction in the area of mining—in the southern Amazon. Thus, neoliberal, natural resource–dependent policies still exist in the country. The Yasuní-ITT proposal, according to President Correa and former CAD member Yolanda Kakabadse, is a step in the right direction, toward post-petroleum policies.

The question of markets and how well they manage the environment is one that is highly debated within the country and even within the transnational networks surrounding the initiative. Alberto Acosta, in his book, *The Curse of Abundance*, argues that the good life can be achieved through initiatives like Yasuní-ITT. He contends that continued discussion between national and international actors in civil society can improve the initiative and correct vague or contrary positions.[24] While inconsistencies in policy at the macro level exist, those involved in the initiative concur with the alternative norms and seek to alter climate change policy nationally and globally through this initiative. Many actors affirm that this is an opportunity at local, national, regional, and global levels to protect biodiversity and demonstrate the social significance of doing so, i.e., protecting indigenous communities.

Institutionalization and Internalization of Norms

The political opportunity structure (POS) for this initiative came from a myriad of levels, including at the global level: 1) the emergence of BRIC (Brazil, Russia, India, and China) economies and their political importance on the international stage; 2) the fallout from the financial crisis and global conversations to rethink post–World War II international institutions and policies; and 3) social learning processes that occurred during the 1990s when many transnational networks formed. At the national and local levels, the new constitution and the support of the initiative from former Minister of Energy and Mines Alberto Acosta and President Rafael Correa have functioned as catalysts to motor the initiative through national politics and international agendas. Furthermore, Ecuadorian NGOs, such as Acción Ecológica and

Fundación Pachamama, no longer seek approval for the alternative norms and how they frame the initiative; rather, they collaborate with their global colleagues to adapt such concepts to international levels.

In the case of institutionalization of the initiative, it began as an idea from civil society and moved over a two-year period to be represented within a new political institution: the CAD. At the global level, the UNDP established a trust fund with Ecuador and various countries have pledged support. The internalization of the norms underlying the initiative is less clear. NGO actors have internalized the norms of post-petroleum politics and economic and political policies toward harmony with nature and the protection of human rights. However, time will tell if Ecuadorian society does the same. Such a test will come when and if the state chooses to extract oil from the Amazon in the ITT block or elsewhere. The president will have to present such a decision for a vote, according to the new constitution. This vote will demonstrate the strength of the alternative norms.

The Counter-Boomerang Effect

The counter-boomerang effect, in which domestic actors initiate a campaign *with* the state government, is illustrative of this campaign. Ultimately, the Ministry of Natural and Cultural Heritage and the CAD assumed responsibility for the initiative and normative change at national and international levels. As illustrated in chapters 4 and 5, the Ecuadorian state initially collaborated closely with NGO representatives and civil society to develop the first version of the initiative. As the initiative matured and developed, institutionalization strengthened and formalized through the CAD. Since the summer of 2009, after less than one year in place, CAD members again reached out to civil society for input on their final version of the proposal. Unlike the boomerang effect of Keck and Sikkink, this process did not include a "violating state."[25] Instead, the state was simultaneously the offending actor and collaborator. As one NGO representative commented, "It was the first time we worked *with* the government on a campaign."[26]

Civil society still plays an active role in shaping the initiative. As Esperanza Martínez noted, "we keep a comfortable distance from the government."[27] While the government process through the CAD works with civil society, collaborating states and organizations, and international meetings, transnational advocacy networks remain both supportive and critical of the initiative. Alberto Acosta argues that this process is one of the democratic orientation of civil society toward the good life—creating a sustainable future for the planet. The process remains political, pressuring the government to continue its quest to keep ITT's oil underground.[28]

The outcome of this counter-boomerang collaboration has so far been successful. A seemingly utopian goal of leaving one of the largest oil reserves underground in a poor country is now an official public policy of the state and has been supported by the United Nations and other collaborating states. The question remains, however, whether the proposal will be successful in capturing funds from the world and if oil ultimately stays underground. In any case, the initiative is already a strong case of changing tides in Latin American politics, as the governments of Bolivia, Brazil, Mexico, and Venezuela have expressed support and interest in the proposal. It is also a strong case for innovative proposals to solve climate change from poor countries. Finally, the global governance processes created by the initiative and the mechanisms for its funding highlight the complexity of international relations and the importance of studying the authority of non-state actors.[29]

Down River: Kyoto and the Future of the Amazon and Our Planet

With only vague commitment on post-2012 climate change agreements from the United States and China, among other leading industrialized nations, the developing world needs to seek solutions now to climate change problems that impact their environments, societies, and future generations. Brazil ranks fourth on the list of the largest carbon emitters in the world.[30] This is due to its extreme level of deforestation, which increased in 2008 and is about 20 percent of its Amazonian rainforest—about the size of Greece.[31] In fact, Brazil is responsible for 48 percent of all deforestation on the planet.[32] Approximately 30 percent of Ecuador's Amazonian region has been deforested.[33] Ecuador's greatest areas of deforestation follow oil access roads.[34] In both cases, deforestation of the Amazon is caused by natural resource extraction, infrastructure projects, and agricultural development, in addition to legal and illegal logging.[35] The consequences of such destruction are catastrophic for our planet, as tree logging releases carbon dioxide into our atmosphere and lost trees are lost sources of natural carbon dioxide absorption for the planet.[36]

In the GEO Ecuador 2008 report, the Ministry of the Environment emphasizes the destruction of biodiversity in the country's rainforest caused by deforestation and reliance on natural resource extraction—namely, oil and mining industries.[37] Researchers directly correlated the rise and fall of Ecuador's GDP with the price of oil from 1980 to 2006.[38] During this time frame, poverty levels in the Amazon increased and environmental threats and degradation rose as well. In conjunction with the Ministry of the Environment and the UNEP, researchers called for a moratorium on oil extraction in the Amazon, which suffers not only from forest loss, but threats to biodiversity and humans as well. In addition, they urged Ecuador to "internalize" international agreements such as the Convention on Biological Diversity, Agenda 21, and the Millennium Development Goals.[39] Given the grim losses in the Amazon, compounded by the violence and threat of loss of indigenous groups, action in this region is necessary for Amazonian countries and citizens of the world alike.

Even though the evidence of destruction and declining oil reserves in the Amazon persists, initiatives continue to build roads and extract natural resources. One such example is the Initiative for Regional Infrastructure Integration (IIRSA). One plan on the drawing board directly impacts the Amazon: the Manta-Manaus project, which would create a transportation system of roads and waterways that would traverse the Amazonian region, beginning in the Brazilian Amazonian city of Manaus, and terminating at the Ecuadorian Pacific port-city of Manta.[40] Researchers like Dr. David Romo of La Universidad San Francisco de Quito and the Tiputini Biodiversity Station in Ecuador's Amazon, among others, call for more coherent policies in the Ecuadorian Amazon where extraction and road building are acceptable in some areas, yet conservation is esteemed in others.[41] While REDD initiatives may abate this level of deforestation, common policies in Amazonian countries are needed.

One sign of hope in this area is the Amazon Cooperation Treaty Organization (OTCA), which includes the eight Amazonian countries (Brazil, Guyana, Suriname, Ecuador, Peru, Colombia, Venezuela, and Bolivia). Aside from a goal of outlining common policies to protect indigenous peoples in the Amazon and the Brazilian Amazon fund (to which Norway has donated $1 billion), no concrete common policies to protect the Amazon have emerged from this organization. Calls to replicate the Yasuní-ITT proposal throughout the Amazon by supporters have been recognized by the OTCA and other member nations, such as Venezuela and Bolivia, but no other Amazonian countries have moved toward such integrative policy or have joined forces with Ecuador to promote the "yasuní-zation" of the area. As REDD policies dominate the conversation of rainforest protection in the UNFCCC negotiations and REDD and REDD+ member states, coordination around the concepts of leaving oil underground to protect forests and payment for avoided emissions will be challenging given the rich resources held by these areas. Ecuadorian officials argue that the Yasuní Fund is a far more comprehensive proposal than REDD, yet also encompasses REDD norms of deforestation prevention and reforestation. While a block of Amazonian countries, led by

Ecuador and Brazil, that support unique initiatives like that of Yasuní-ITT might create a political force within UNFCCC negotiations, state interests in natural resource extraction in this region currently outweigh interests to leave such precious commodities underground.

While researchers have found the Western Amazon to be the richest in terms of biodiversity, they have also found this region the most threatened from oil concessions. One hundred eighty oil concessions spot the map in this area of the rainforest. Peru in 2008 added sixteen blocks to its forty-eight oil blocks, totaling sixty-four oil concessions in its rainforest. According to Matt Finer, a scientist for Save America's Forests,

> Peru is the most troubling country in the region in terms of oil and gas activities. The situations in Ecuador and Bolivia are certainly cause for alarm, but the scope and pace of the recent proliferation of oil and gas concessions in Peru is unprecedented. The vast majority of the Colombian Amazon, on the other hand, is not currently threatened by hydrocarbon activities, presumably because of the dangers posed by the FARC.
>
> Given the large amount of oil and gas known and suspected to lie under the Amazon, and the subsequent build up of hydrocarbon concessions, Ecuador's Yasuní-ITT Initiative is really one of the last hopes for a lot of areas. If it works, it may serve as precedent for similar conflict zones, like Bolivia's Madidi National Park. If it doesn't work, there is not much else to hold governments back from drilling.[42]

It seems as though Ecuadorians are not the only ones seeking the good life. In his book, *Our Choice: A Plan to Solve the Climate Crisis*, Al Gore creates such a roadmap. He might sound like an unlikely candidate to criticize capitalist markets, given his status as former vice president of the United States—the world's beacon of capitalism—but he argues that today's capital markets focus too much on short-term benefits over long-term sustainable growth. He contends that "Business and markets cannot operate in isolation from society or the environment."[43] In the end, he applauds the success of a planetary plan beyond Kyoto not just for current leaders, but for the "generations that follow."[44] Such reasoning is the pursuit of the good life in global terms. The Yasuní-ITT proposal may call the world to protect only one small plot of rainforest, but its ramifications are much larger. It is an innovative and imaginative guide to future ways to protect areas that mean so much to local peoples and the global citizenry. While today the economic and environmental benefits of avoiding emissions and pursuing energy sources beyond oil may seem clear, the wealth of the Amazon lies in what has not yet been discovered. The Yasuní-ITT Initiative is also a tipping point in the natural history of the planet.

Notes

1. Paul J. Nelson and Ellen Dorsey, *New Rights Advocacy: Changing Strategies of Development and Human Rights NGOs* (Washington, D.C.: Georgetown University Press, 2008), 21.

2. Ibid.

3. Ibid.

4. Thomas Risse-Kappen, *Bringing Transnational Relations Back In: Non-state Actors, Domestic Structures, and International Institutions* (Cambridge: Cambridge University Press, 1995); Margaret E. Keck and Kathryn Sikkink, *Activists beyond Borders: Advocacy Networks in International Politics* (Ithaca, NY: Cornell University Press, 1998).

5. Nelson and Dorsey, *New Rights Advocacy.*

6. Iniciativa Yasuní-ITT, Ministry of Natural and Cultural Patrimony, Sección Noticias, http://yasuni-itt.gob.ec/blog/seccion/noticias/ (accessed December 15, 2010).

7. Memo from German minister of economic development and cooperation Dirk Niebel to representative Ute Koczy regarding the Yasuní-ITT Initiative, September 14, 2010 (unpublished memo).

8. "Presidente de Ecuador promoverá Iniciativa Yasuní en Cancún, *Radio Sucre,* December 6, 2010, http://www.radiosucre.com.ec/index.php?option=com_content& view=article&id=8910:presidente-de-ecuador-promovera-iniciativa-yasuni-en -cancun-&catid=1:politica&Itemid=24.

9. Yolanda Kakabadse, interviews, Quito, Ecuador, January 21, and April 13, 2009.

10. Elinor Ostrom and Emilio Moran, eds. *Seeing the Forest and the Trees: Human-Environment Interactions in Forest Ecosystems* (Cambridge, MA: MIT Press, 2005).

11. Robert Putnam, *Making Democracy Work* (Princeton, NJ: Princeton University, 1993).

12. Matt Finer, Save America's Forests, e-mail to author, December 3, 2009; Save America's Forests also facilitated the participation of Waorani leaders in the November 2007 Yasuní-ITT conference in Quito.

13. "Encuesta de Percepción Ciudadana Francisco de Orellana," Grupo Faro (unpublished survey data received via e-mail to author).

14. "Correa firmó ayer amplio pacto económico con Rusia," *El Universo,* October 30, 2009.

15. Interviews with various NGOs in Washington, D.C., after a visit with CAD officials, November 2009.

16. Financial Action Task Force, public statement, February 10, 2010, http://www .fatf-gafi.org/dataoecd/34/29/44636171.pdf.

17. Suzanne Goldenberg, "US Denies Climate Aid to Countries Opposing Copenhagen Accord: Bolivia and Ecuador Will Be Denied Aid after Both Opposed the Accord," *Guardian,* April 9, 2010, http://www.guardian.co.uk/environment/2010/ apr/09/us-climate-aid.

18. Alberto Acosta, *La Maldición de la Abundancia* (Quito, Ecuador: Abya Yala, 2009); Fander Falconí and Carlos M. Larrea, "Impactos ambientales de las políticas

de liberalización externa y los flujos de capital: el caso de Ecuador," in *Globalización y Desarrollo en América Latina*, ed. Fander Falconí, Marcelo Hercowitz, and Roldan Muradian (Quito, Ecuador: FLACSO, 2004).

19. "Megadiverse countries are located between the tropics of Cancer and Capricorn, where tropical forests are concentrated. These countries host most of the planet's biodiversity and have significant fossil fuel reserves in highly biologically and culturally sensitive areas. Among the countries that fulfill all of these conditions are: Brazil, Colombia, Costa Rica, Democratic Republic of Congo, Ecuador, India, Indonesia, Madagascar, Malaysia, Papua New Guinea, Peru, Bolivia, the Philippines and Venezuela. The United Nations Environment Programme (UNEP) has designated 19 countries in the world as megadiverse," *Yasuní-ITT Initiative*, 30, http://www.yasuni-itt.gov.ec/download/Yasuni_ITT_Initiative1009.pdf.

20. "Secretario General de la ONU interesado en Yasuní-ITT," Ecuador Inmediato Noticias, http://ns2.ecuadorinmediato.com/index.php?module=Noticias&func=news _user_view&id=116354&umt=Nuevo%20embajador%20de%20Ecuador%20ante%20 la%20ONU%20presenta%20credenciales%20a%20Ban%20Ki-moon.

21. Naomi Mapstone, "Ecuador Reaches Deal with Most Oil Companies," *Financial Times*, November 24, 2010, http://www.ft.com/cms/s/0/ac2581f4-f766-11df -8b42-00144feab49a.html#axzz1AAeDmJRb (accessed December 10, 2010).

22. Carl Ross, interview, November 12, 2009.

23. Jeffrey Checkel, "Why Comply? Social Learning and European Identity Change," *International Organization* 55, no. 3 (Summer 2001): 553–588.

24. Acosta, *La Maldición de la Abundancia*, 184.

25. Keck and Sikkink, *Activists beyond Borders*; Nelson and Dorsey, *New Rights Advocacy*.

26. Interview with author, 2009.

27. Interview with author, 2009.

28. Acosta, *La Maldición de la Abundancia*, 184.

29. See also Claire Cutler et al., *Private Authority and International Affairs* (Albany, NY: SUNY Press, 1999); and Rodney Hall and Thomas J. Biersteker, "The Emergence of Private Authority in the International System," in *The Emergence of Private Authority in Global Governance*, ed. Rodney Bruce Hall and Thomas J. Biersteker (Cambridge: Cambridge University Press, 2002).

30. Al Gore, *Our Choice: A Plan to Solve the Climate Crisis* (Emmaus, PA: Rodale Publishers, 2009), 173.

31. Rhett Butler, "Deforestation in the Amazon," *Mongabay*, http://www.mongabay .com/brazil.html (accessed October 24, 2009).

32. Gore, *Our Choice*, 174.

33. Jefferson Mecham, "Causes and Consequences of Deforestation in Ecuador;" Centro de Investigación de los Bosques Tropicales, CIBT, May 2001; Sven Wunder, *The Economics of Deforestation: The Example of Ecuador* (Basingstoke, UK: Macmillan Press, 2000).

34. Matt Finer et al., "Oil and Gas Projects in the Western Amazon: Threats to Wilderness, Biodiversity, and Indigenous Peoples," *PLoS ONE* 3, no. 8 (2008): 2.

35. Gore, *Our Choice*, 173–175; Butler, "Deforestation in the Amazon."

36. Joseph Henry Vogel, "No abrir nuevas carreteras: una directriz práctica para aliviar la pérdida de biodiversidad en la Amazonía," in *La economía ecológica: una nueva mirada a la ecología humana*, ed. Tania Ricardi (La Paz, Bolivia: CESU-UMSS/ UNESCO, Plural Editores, 1999), 443–461.

37. Guillaume Fontaine, Iván Narváez, and Paúl Cisneros, eds., *GEO Ecuador 2008: Informe sobre el estado del medio ambiente* (Quito, Ecuador: UNDP and FLACSO, 2008), 16.

38. Ibid., 26.

39. Ibid., 148–154.

40. "Correa aboga por carretera Manta-Manaos," *El Universo*, September 20, 2009.

41. David Romo, interview, March 25, 2009.

42. Matt Finer, e-mail to author, 2009.

43. Gore, *Our Choice*, 346.

44. Ibid., 404.

Bibliography

Acosta, Alberto. *Desarrollo Glocal: Con la Amazonia en la Mira.* Quito: Corporación Editora Nacional, 2005.
———. "El Buen Vivir, una oportunidad por construir." Portal de Economía Solidaria, February 17, 2009.
———. "El petróleo en el Ecuador: Una evaluación crítica del pasado cuarto del siglo." In *El Ecuador Post Petrolero,* 3–33. Quito, Ecuador: Acción Ecológica, Idlis, and Oilwatch, 2000.
———. *La Maldición de la Abundancia.* Quito, Ecuador: Abya Yala, 2009.
Acosta, Alberto, Eduardo Gudynas, Esperanza Martínez, and Joseph Henry Vogel. "A Political, Economic, and Ecological Initiative in the Ecuadorian Amazon." Americas Program Policy Report, August 13, 2009.
Acosta, Alberto, and Esperanza Martínez. *El Buen Vivir: Una vía para el desarrollo.* Quito, Ecuador: Abya Yala, 2009.
Aldy, Joseph E., and Robert N. Stavins. *Post-Kyoto International Climate Policy: Summary for Policymakers.* Cambridge: Cambridge University Press, 2009.
Amazon Fund. "The Amazon Is the Lungs of the Planet: As the Amazon Goes, so Goes the Planet." http://www.amazonfund.org/index.php (accessed October 25, 2009).
Andonova, Liliana B., Michele M. Betsill, and Harriet Bulkeley. "Transnational Climate Governance." *Global Environmental Politics* 9, no. 2: 52–73.
Bandy, Joe, and Jackie Smith, eds. *Coalitions across Borders: Transnational Protest and the Neoliberal Order.* Lanham, MD: Rowman and Littlefield, 2005.
Bass, Margot S., Matt Finer, Clinton N. Jenkins, Holger Kreft, Diego F. Cisneros-Heredia, et al. "Global Conservation Significance of Ecuador's Yasuní National Park." *PLoS ONE* 5, no. 1 (2010): e8767. doi:10.1371/journal.pone.0008767.
Beckerman, Stephen, Pamela I. Erickson, James Yost, Jhanira Regalado, Lilia Jaramillo, Corey Sparks, Moises Iromenga, and Kathryn Long. "Life Histories, Blood

Revenge, and Reproductive Success among the Waorani of Ecuador." *Proceedings of the National Academy of Sciences of the United States* 107, no. 45 (2010): 19195–19200.

Bettelheim, Eric. "Yasuni's Means Won't Achieve Its Ends." The Katoomba Group's Ecosystem Marketplace, August 27, 2009.

Bob, Clifford. *The Marketing of Rebellion: Insurgents, Media, and International Activism.* Cambridge: Cambridge University Press, 2005.

Brysk, Allison. *From Tribal Village to Global Village: Indian Rights and International Relations in Latin America.* Stanford, CA: Stanford University Press, 2000.

Butler, Rhett. "Deforestation in the Amazon." Mongabay. http://www.mongabay .com/brazil.html (accessed October 24, 2009).

Cabodevilla, Miguel Angel. "Pueblos ocultos en Ecuador." *Llacta!* November 2006. http://www.llacta.org/textos/yasuni016.html.

Carpenter, Charli R. "Studying Issue (Non)-Adoption in Transnational Advocacy Networks." *International Organization* 61, no. 3 (2007): 643–667.

Checkel, Jeffrey T. "Why Comply? Social Learning and European Identity Change." *International Organization* 55, no. 3 (Summer 2001): 553–588.

Climate Focus. "Análisis Legal y Financiero de la Implementación de la Iniciativa ITT-Yasuní," 2009, http://www.yasuni-itt.gov.ec/download/Reporte_Legal_Climate _Focus.pdf.

Conca, Ken. *Governing Water: Contentious Transnational Politics and Global Institution Building.* Cambridge, MA: MIT Press, 2006.

Corporación Financiera Nacional. Los Certificados de Garantía Yasuní y el Fideicomiso Mercantil de Transformación Energética, January 9, 2008.

Correa, Rafael. "Speech of the President of Ecuador; High Level Dialogue on Climate Change of the 62nd Period of Sessions of the General Assembly of the United Nations," September 24, 2007. http://www.ecuador.org/bulletin_board/relative_docs/ letter_climatechange.pdf.

———. "Yasuní-ITT." http://www.youtube.com/user/YasuniITT#p/a/f/0/ _dg48IM9gwM. Last modified May 30, 2009 (accessed December 20, 2009).

Crespo, Ricardo. "La legislación contradictoria sobre conservación y explotación petrolera." In *Yasuní en el siglo XXI: El Estado ecuatoriano y la conservación en la Amazonía,* edited by Guillaume Fontaine and Iván Navráez, 207–222. Quito, Ecuador: Abya Yala, 2007.

Cutler, Claire A., Virginia Haufler, and Tony Porter. *Private Authority and International Affairs.* Albany, NY: SUNY Press, 1999.

Daly, Herman. Section 1, chapter 1 of Agenda 21 (International Policies to Accelerate Sustainable Development in Developing Countries and Related Domestic Policies). *Population and Environment* 15, no. 1 (September 1993): 66–69.

DeMars, William E. *NGOs and Transnational Networks: Wild Cards in World Politics.* London: Pluto Press, 2005.

Energy Information Administration. "Crude Oil and Total Petroleum Imports Top 15 Countries," September 29, 2009. http://www.eia.doe.gov/pub/oil_gas/petroleum/ data_publications/company_level_imports/current/import.html.

Falconí, Fander, and Carlos M. Larrea. "Impactos ambientales de las políticas de liberalización externa y los flujos de capital: el caso de Ecuador." In *Globalización y Desarrollo en América Latina*, edited by Fander Falconí, Marcelo Hercowitz, and Roldan Muradian, 133–154. Quito, Ecuador: FLACSO, 2004.

Financial Action Task Force. Public statement, February 10, 2010. http://www.fatf-gafi .org/dataoecd/34/29/44636171.pdf.

Finer, Matt M. "Ecuador Seeks Compensation to Leave Amazon Oil Undisturbed." *Environment News Service*, April 24, 2007. http://www.llacta.org/textos/yasuni016 .html.

Finer, Matt, C. N. Jenkins, S. L. Pimm, B. Keane, and C. Ross. "Oil and Gas Projects in the Western Amazon: Threats to Wilderness, Biodiversity, and Indigenous Peoples." *PLoS ONE* 3, no. 8 (2008): e2932. doi:10.1371/journal.pone.0002932.

Finer, Matt, and Pamela Martin. "Ecuador's Amazon-sized Challenge to the World: Part I." *Globalist*. http://www.theglobalist.com/storyid.aspx?StoryId=8527 (accessed on December 12, 2010).

Finer, Matt, Varsha Vijay, Fernando Ponce, Clinton Jenkins, and Ted Kahn. "Ecuador's Yasuní Biosphere Reserve: A Brief Modern History and Conservation Challenges." *IOP Publishing Environmental Research*, July–September 2009. doi:10.1088/1748-9326/4/3/034005.

Finger, Matthias. "Which Governance for Sustainable Development? An Organizational and Institutional Perspective." In *The Crisis of Global Environmental Governance: Towards a New Political Economy of Sustainability*, edited by Jacob Park, Ken Conca, and Matthias Finger, 34–57. New York: Routledge, 2008.

Finnemore, Martha. "Norms, Culture and World Politics: Insights from Sociology's Institutionalism." *International Organization* 50, no. 2 (Spring 1996): 325–347

Flavin, Christopher, and Robert Engelman. "The Perfect Storm." In *2009 State of the World: Into a Warming World: A Worldwatch Institute Report on Progress toward a Sustainable Society*, edited by Linda Starke, 5–12. New York: W. W. Norton, 2009.

Fontaine, Guillaume. *El Precio del Petróleo*. Quito, Ecuador: Abya Yala, 2007.

Fontaine, Guillaume, and Iván Narváez, eds. *Yasuní en el siglo XXI: El Estado ecuatoriano y la conservación de la Amazonía*. Quito, Ecuador: FLACSO, 2007.

Fontaine, Guillame, Iván Narváez, and Paúl Cisneros, eds. *GEO Ecuador 2008: Informe sobre el Estado del Medio Ambiente*. Quito, Ecuador: UNDP and FLACSO, 2008.

Forbes.com. "Ecuador Remittances Fall 21 pct in First 6 Months." http://www.forbes .com/feeds/ap/2009/08/17/ap6787416.html (accessed October 25, 2009).

Friedman, Thomas L. "The First Law of Petro Politics." *Foreign Policy*, May–June 2006, 29–36.

Giddens, Anthony. *Runaway World: How Globalizing Is Reshaping Our Lives*. New York: Routledge, 2000.

Gills, Barry K. *Globalization and Global History. London*. New York: Routledge, 2005.

Global Carbon Project. "Carbon Budget and Trends 2007," September 26, 2008. www .globalcarbonproject.org.

Gore, Al. *Our Choice: A Plan to Solve the Climate Crisis*. Emmaus, PA: Rodale Publishers, 2009.

Government of Ecuador. Decreto Ejecutivo 847. Quito, Ecuador. January 2, 2008.
———. Decreto Ejecutivo 882. Quito, Ecuador. January 21, 2008.
———. Decreto Ejecutivo 1227. Quito, Ecuador. July 29, 2008.
———. Decreto Ejecutivo 1572. Quito, Ecuador. February 5, 2009.
Gudynas, Eduardo. *Ecología, Economía y Ética del Desarrollo Sostenible.* Quito, Ecuador: Abya Yala, 2003.
———. *El Mandato Ecológico: Derechos de la naturaleza y políticas ambientales en la nueva Constitución.* Quito, Ecuador: Abya Yala, 2009.
———. "Seis puntos clave en ambiente y desarrollo." In *El Buen Vivir: Una vía para el desarrollo,* edited by Alberto Acosta and Esperanza Martínez, 39–50. Quito, Ecuador: Abya Yala, 2009.
Haas, Peter M. "Do Regimes Matter? Epistemic Communities and Mediterranean Pollution Control." *International Organization* 43, no. 3 (Summer 1989): 377–403.
Hall, Rodney, and Thomas J. Biersteker. "The Emergence of Private Authority in the International System." In *The Emergence of Private Authority in Global Governance,* edited by Rodney Hall and Thomas J. Biersteker, 3–22. Cambridge: Cambridge University Press, 2002.
Hall, Thomas D., and Christopher Chase-Dunn. "Global Social Change in the Long Run." In *Global Social Change: Historical and Comparative Perspectives,* 33–58. Baltimore, MD: Johns Hopkins University Press, 2006.
Hare, W. L. "A Safe Landing for the Climate." In *2009 State of the World: Into a Warming World: A Worldwatch Institute Report on Progress toward a Sustainable Society,* edited by Linda Starke, 13–29. New York: W. W. Norton, 2009.
Hawken, Paul. *Blessed Unrest: How the Largest Social Movement in History Is Restoring Grace, Justice, and Beauty to the World.* New York: Penguin, 2007.
Held, David, and Anthony McGrew. *Globalization/Anti-Globalization.* Oxford: Polity, 2002.
Hochstetler, Kathryn, and Margaret E. Keck. *Greening Brazil.* Durham, NC: Duke University Press, 2007.
Human Rights Council. "Expert Mechanism on the Rights of Indigenous Peoples," June 30, 2009. http://www2.ohchr.org/english/issues/indigenous/ExpertMechanism/2nd/docs/A_HRC_EMRIP_2009_6.pdf.
"Imposible no contagiarse del entusiasmo del Yasuní ITT: Presidente Correa." *Diario Hoy.* May 30, 2009. http://www.hoy.com.ec/noticias-ecuador/proyecto-itt-avanza-maravilloso-dice-correa-351083.html.
Iniciativa Yasuní-ITT. "Apoyo Internacional Recibido." http://www.llacta.org/notic/2007/not0524c.htm (accessed November 15, 2009).
———. "El Presidente Correa se refiere a la Iniciativa Yasuní-ITT durante la posesión." August 18, 2009. http://www.youtube.com/watch?v=1B08eSjn1hc&feature=related.
———. "Letter about Proposed Petrobras Road into Yasuní National Park." November 25, 2004. http://www.tadpoleorg.org/files/English_Letter_and_Report.pdf.
———. "Mesa redonda en la FLACSO." http://www.youtube.com/watch?v=4iXbIyqAilk (accessed September 16, 2009).

———. "Otras propuestas Internacionales." http://yasuni-itt.gob.ec/preguntas-y
-respuestas/otras-propuestas-internacionales/ (accessed December 14, 2010).

———. "Yasuní-ITT en la agenda internacional del Ecuador." http://yasuni-itt.gob.ec/
preguntas-y-respuestas/los-apoyos/ (accessed December 14, 2010).

Jackson, Tim. *Prosperity without Growth: The Transition to a Sustainable Economy.*
London: Sustainable Development Commission, 2010.

Keck, Margaret E., and Kathryn Sikkink. *Activists beyond Borders: Advocacy Networks
in International Politics.* Ithaca, NY: Cornell University Press, 1998.

Keohane, Robert O., and Joseph S. Nye. *Transnational Relations and World Politics.*
Cambridge, MA: MIT Press, 1971.

Khagram, Sanjeev, James Riker, and Kathryn Sikkink, eds. *Restructuring World Politics: Transnational Social Movements, Networks and Norms.* Minneapolis: University
of Minnesota Press, 2002.

Khagram, Sanjeev, and Saleem H. Ali. "Transnational Transformations: From
Government-centric Interstate Regimes to Cross-sectoral Multi-level Networks of
Global Governance." In *The Crisis of Global Governance: Toward a New Political
Economy of Sustainability,* edited by Jacob Park, Ken Conca, and Matthias Finger,
132–162. New York: Routledge, 2008.

Kimmerling, Judith. *Amazon Crude.* New York: Natural Resources Defense Council,
1991.

Krasner, Stephen D. "Structural Causes and Regime Consequences: Regimes as Intervening Variables." In *International Regimes.* Ithaca, NY: Cornell University Press,
1982.

Lander, Edgardo. "Hacia otra noción de riqueza." In *El Buen Vivir: Una vía para el
desarrollo,*" edited by Alberto Acosta and Esperanza Martínez. Quito, Ecuador:
Abya Yala, 2009.

Langewiesche, William. "Jungle Law." *Vanity Fair,* May 4, 2007. http://www.vanityfair
.com/politics/features/2007/05/texaco200705.

Larrea, Carlos. "Resumen expo COICA," August 20, 2009. http://www.youtube.com/
watch?v=tqRCOiZTfNo.

Larrea, Carlos, Natalia Greene, Laura Rival, Elisa Sevilla, and Lavinia Warnars. "Yasuní-ITT Initiative a Big Idea from a Small Country," October 2009. http://www
.yasuni-itt.gov.ec/download/Yasuni_ITT_Initiative1009.pdf.

Larsen Maher, Julie. "Oil and Wildlife Don't Mix in Ecuador's Eden." Wildlife Conservation Society/Physorg.com, September 10, 2009.

Le Quang, Matthieu. "La moratoria petrolífera en la Amazonía ecuatoriana, una propuesta inspiradora para la Cumbre de Copenhague." *Boletin ECOS* 8 (September
10, 2009): 1–23.

Lipschutz, Ronnie D., and Judith Mayer. *Global Civil Society and Global Environmental Governance: The Politics of Nature from Place to Planet.* Albany: State University
of New York, 1996.

Lövbrand, Eva, Teresia Rindefjäll, and Joakim Nordqvist. "Closing the Legitimacy
Gap in Global Environmental Governance?" *Global Environmental Politics* 9, no. 2
(May 2009): 74–100.

Lovejoy, Thomas. "Climate Change's Pressures on Biodiversity." In *2009 State of the World: Into a Warming World: A Worldwatch Institute Report on Progress toward a Sustainable Society*, edited by Linda Starke. New York: W. W. Norton, 2009.

Martin, Pamela. "Ecuador's Biodiverse Paradise Could Still Be Lost to Oil." *Environmental News Service*, February 16, 2010. http://www.ens-newswire.com/ens/feb2010/2010-02-16-02.html.

———. *The Globalization of Contentious Politics: The Amazonian Indigenous Rights Movement*. New York: Routledge, 2003.

Martin, Pamela L., and Franke Wilmer. "Transnational Normative Struggles and Globalization: The Case of Indigenous Peoples in Bolivia and Ecuador." *Globalizations* 5, no. 4 (December 2008): 583–598.

Martínez, Esperanza. "Dejar el Crudo en Tierra en el Yasuní—Un Reto a la Coherencia." *Revista Tendencia* 9 (April 2009): 1–13.

———. "De Kyoto a Quito." *Llacta! Acción Ecológica*, May 9, 2007. http://www.llacta .org/organiz/coms/2007/com0096.htm.

———. "Yasuní: Más de 100 Buenas Razones para NO Sacar el Petróleo." *Amazonía por la Vida*, Quito, Ecuador, November 2008.

Martínez Alier, Joan. "El rol de la economía ecológica en América Latina." In *Globalización y Desarrollo en América Latina*, edited by Fander Falconí, Marcelo Hercowitz, and Roldan Muradian, 11–14. Quito, Ecuador: FLACSO, 2004.

McKibben, Bill. *Deep Economy: The Wealth of Communities and the Future*. New York: Times Books, 2007.

Mecham, Jefferson. "Causes and Consequences of Deforestation in Ecuador." Centro de Investigación de los Bosques Tropicales—CIBT. May 2001.

Metz, B., O. R. Davidson, P. R. Bosch, R. Dave, and L. A. Meyer, eds. *Climate Change 2007: Mitigation. Contribution of Working Group III to the Fourth Assessment Report of the Intergovernmental Panel on Climate Change*. IPCC. New York: Cambridge University Press, 2007.

Ministerio de Relaciones Exteriores, Comercio e Integración. "Encuentro Taller-Iniciativa Yasuní-ITT." Vicepresidencia de la República, Ministerio de Relaciones Exteriores, Comercio e Integración, Universidad Andina Simón Bolívar, Earth Economics, World Resources Institute, November 21–23, 2007. http://www.eartheconomics.org/FileLibrary/file/Reports/Summary_of_Yasun%C3%AD_ITT_Conference.pdf.

Narváez, Iván. "La política ambiental del Estado: Hacia el colapso del modelo de conservación?" In *Yasuní en el siglo XXI: El Estado ecuatoriano y la conservación en la Amazonía*, edited by Guillaume Fontaine and Iván Narváez. Quito, Ecuador: Abya Yala, 2007.

Nelson, Paul J., and Ellen Dorsey. *New Rights Advocacy: Changing Strategies of Development and Human Rights NGOs*. Washington, D.C.: Georgetown University Press, 2008.

O'Brien, Robert, Anne Marie Goetz, Jan Aart Scholte, and Marc Williams. *Contesting Global Governance: Multilateral Economic Institutions and Global Social Movements*. Cambridge: Cambridge University Press, 2000.

Okereke, Chukwumerije, and Harriet Buklekey. "Conceptualizing Climate Change Governance beyond the International Regime: A Review of Four Theoretical Approaches." *Tyndall Centre for Climate Change Research*. http://www.tyndall.ac.uk/publications/working_papers/twp112.pdf.

Organización de Tratado de Cooperación Amazónica. "Declaración de los Jefes de Estado sobre la Organización." http://www.otca.org.br/publicacao/SPT-TCA-ECU-20.pdf.

Ortiz T., Pablo. *Globalización y Conflictos Socioambientales*. Quito, Ecuador: Abya Yala, 1997.

Ostrom, Elinor, and Emilio Moran, eds. *Seeing the Forest and the Trees: Human-Environment Interactions in Forest Ecosystems*. Cambridge, MA: MIT Press, 2005.

Princen, Thomas. *The Logic of Sufficiency*. Cambridge, MA: MIT Press, 2005.

Princen, Thomas, Michael Maniates, and Ken Conca, eds. *Confronting Consumption*. Cambridge, MA: MIT Publishers, 2000.

Putnam, Robert D. *Making Democracy Work: Civic Traditions in Modern Italy*. Princeton, NJ: Princeton University, 1993.

Risse-Kappen, Thomas. *Bringing Transnational Relations Back In: Non-state Actors, Domestic Structures, and International Institutions*. Cambridge: Cambridge University Press, 1995.

Risse-Kappen, Thomas, Stephen C. Ropp, and Kathryn Sikkink. *The Power of Human Rights: International Norms and Domestic Change*. Cambridge: Cambridge University Press, 1999.

Risse-Kappen, Thomas, and Kathryn Sikkink. "The Socialization of International Human Rights Norms into Domestic Practices: Introduction." In *The Power of Human Rights: International Norms and Domestic Change*, ed. Thomas Risse-Kappen, Stephen C. Ropp, and Kathryn Sikkink. Cambridge: Cambridge University Press, 1999.

Rival, Laura. *Trekking thru History*. Cambridge: Cambridge University Press, 2002.

Rosenau, James N. *Along the Domestic-Foreign Frontier: Exploring Governance in a Turbulent World*. Cambridge: Cambridge University Press, 1997.

——. *Distant Proximities: Dynamics beyond Globalization*. Princeton, NJ: Princeton University Press, 2003.

——. *People Count! Networked Individuals in Global Politics*. Boulder, CO: Paradigm Publishers, 2008.

Ross, Michael L. "Does Oil Hinder Democracy?" *World Politics* 53, no. 3 (April 2001): 325–361.

Scholte, Jan Aart. "Civil Society and Democracy in Global Governance." *Global Governance* 8, no. 3 (July–Sept 2002): 281–306.

Scientists Concerned for Yasuní. November 24, 2004. http://saveamericasforests.org/Yasuni/Science/SciConcrndfrYasuni.pdf.

Sevilla, Roque. "The Yasuní-ITT: An Innovative Model to Save the Planet." Presentation, November 2008.

Shankleman, Jill. *Oil, Profits, and Peace: Does Business Have a Role in Peacemaking?* Washington, D.C.: United States Institute of Peace, 2006.

Sikkink, Kathryn. "Patterns of Dynamic Multilevel Governance and the Insider-Outsider Coalition." In *Transnational Protest and Global Activism*, edited by Donatella Della Porta and Sidney Tarrow, 151–173. New York: Rowman and Littlefield, 2005.

Silvestrum VoF. "Análisis de la Iniciativa ITT-Yasuní frente a los Mercados de carbono." June 10, 2009.

———. "Analysis of the ITT-Yasuní Initiative vis à vis Carbon Markets." May 12, 2009.

Sklair, Leslie F. *Globalization, Capitalism, and Its Alternatives.* Oxford: Oxford University Press, 2002.

Speth, James Gustave. *The Bridge at the Edge of the World.* New Haven, CT: Yale University Press, 2008.

Speth, James Gustave, and Peter M. Haas. *Global Environmental Governance.* Washington, D.C.: Island Press, 2006.

Tarrow, Sidney. *The New Transnational Activism.* Cambridge: Cambridge University Press, 2005.

Tetreault, Mary Ann, and Ronnie D. Lipschutz. *Global Politics as if People Mattered.* Lanham, MD: Rowman and Littlefield, 2005.

Tilly, Charles. *From Mobilization to Revolution.* New York: McGraw Hill Publishing, 1978.

"United Nations Human Development Index 2010 Rankings." United Nations Development Program. http://hdr.undp.org/en/statistics/.

UN-REDD Programme Fund. "Secretary-General and Prime Minister of Norway Launch UN-REDD Programme." http://www.undp.org/mdtf/un-redd/overview .shtml.

Vogel, Joseph Henry. *The Economics of the Yasuní Initiative: Climate Change as if Thermodynamics Mattered.* London: Anthem Press, 2009.

———. "No abrir nuevas carreteras: una directriz práctica para aliviar la pérdida de biodiversidad en la Amazonía." In *La economía ecológica: una nueva mirada a la ecología humana,* edited by Tania Ricardi, 443–461. La Paz, Bolivia: CESU-UMSS/ UNESCO, Plural Editores.

von Bülow, Michael. "World Bank: Poor Countries Will Be Hit Hardest." United Nations Climate Change Conference, December 7–18, 2009. November 5, 2009. http://en.cop15.dk/news/view+news?newsid=2272.

Wapner, Paul. *Environmental Activism and World Civic Politics.* Albany, NY: SUNY, 1996.

Wendt, Alexander E. "The Agent-Structure Problem in International Relations Theory." *International Organization* 41, no. 3 (1987): 236–370.

Wolf, Martin. "Will the Nation State Survive Globalization?" *Foreign Affairs* 80, no. 1 (February 2001): 178–190.

Wood, Leslie J. "Bridging the Chasms: The Case of Peoples' Global Action." In *Coalitions across Borders: Transnational Protest and the Neoliberal Order,* edited by Joe Bandy and Jackie Smith, 95–120. Lanham, MD: Rowman and Littlefield, 2005.

Wunder, Sven. *The Economics of Deforestation: The Example of Ecuador.* Basingstoke, UK: Macmillan Press, 2000.

———. *Oil Wealth and the Fate of the Forest: A Comparative Study of Eight Tropical Countries.* New York: Routledge, 2003.

Index

About the Author

Pamela Martin is an associate professor of politics and international relations at Coastal Carolina University in Myrtle Beach, South Carolina. She is also the director of the International and Global Studies Minor, as well as advisor to the Model United Nations Club. Dr. Martin researched the Yasuní-ITT Initiative and its global governance mechanisms on a Fulbright Scholar award in Ecuador in 2009. Her research areas include global governance, environmental politics, energy, and transnational networks. Dr. Martin received her Ph.D. from the University of Maryland, College Park, and taught at La Universidad San Francisco de Quito, Ecuador, prior to returning to the United States in 1998.